SCRIPTURE UNION

BIBLE CHARACTERS AND DOCTRINES

Elkanah to David
E. M. BLAIKLOCK, M.A., D.Litt.

The Holy Trinity
GEOFFREY GROGAN, B.D., M.Th.

SCRIPTURE UNION
5 WIGMORE STREET
LONDON, W1H0AD

© 1972 Scripture Union
First published 1972

I SBN 0 85421 307 4

Printed and bound in Ireland by
Cahill & Co. Limited, Dublin

Scripture Union Bible Characters and Doctrines

INTRODUCTION

This series of S.U. Bible study aids takes its place alongside
our existing range of Notes and Bible Study Books.

Each volume of Bible Characters and Doctrines is divided
into the right number of sections to make daily use possible,
though dates are not attached to the sections because of the
books' continuing use as a complete set of character studies
and doctrinal expositions. The study for each day is clearly
numbered and the Bible passage to be read is placed alongside
it.

Sections presenting the characters and doctrines alternate
throughout each book, providing balance and variety in the
selected subjects. At the end of each section there is a selection
of questions and themes for further study related to the
material covered in the preceding readings.

Each volume will provide material for one quarter's use,
with between 91 and 96 sections. Where it is suggested that
two sections should be read together in order to fit the three-
month period, they are marked with an asterisk.

The scheme will be completed in four years. Professor E.
M. Blaiklock, who writes all the character studies, will work
progressively through the Old and New Testament records.
Writers of the doctrinal sections contribute to a pattern of
studies drawn up by the Rev. Geoffrey Grogan, Principal of
the Bible Training Institute, Glasgow, in his capacity as
Co-ordinating Editor. A chart overleaf indicates how the
doctrinal sections are planned.

In this series biblical quotations are normally taken from
the RSV unless otherwise identified. Occasionally Professor
Blaiklock provides his own translation of the biblical text.

DOCTRINAL STUDY SCHEME

	Year 1	Year 2	Year 3	Year 4
First Quarter	The God who Speaks	Man and Sin	The Work of Christ	The Kingdom and the Church
Second Quarter	God in His World	Law and Grace	Righteousness in Christ	The Mission of the Church
Third Quarter	The Character of God	The Life of Christ	Life in Christ	The Church's Ministry and Ordinances
Fourth Quarter	The Holy Trinity	The Person of Christ	The Holy Spirit	The Last Things

4

DOCTRINAL STUDIES
THE HOLY TRINITY

Study

Study

Plurality in Unity (N.T. History)

Plurality in Unity (N.T. Epistles)

Three in One (Part 1)

Three in One (Part 2)

CHARACTER STUDIES
ELKANAH TO DAVID

Study

Study

THE HOLY TRINITY

INTRODUCTION

The Christian doctrine of the Trinity is often regarded as a mystery which is beyond understanding and which the ordinary Christian should leave to the professional theologian. It is true that it is a mystery but should we be surprised by this? God is our Creator. He fashioned this great universe with all its complexity. He the Creator must be far greater than His universe, and there is much about the universe which we cannot understand. How surprising if we were able to comprehend the Being of its Creator and encounter no mystery as we consider Him! This mystery baffles the intellect but it causes the Christian to worship—and not least the professional theologian!

Do not regard this doctrine as a burden to faith but as an aid to it. It has great devotional value. I kneel to pray. I am in communion with the great and holy God, the Creator of the universe. Put in these terms He may seem remote to me, but the Lord Jesus has taught me to call Him 'Father'. Moreover, this great God has manifested Himself in the Lord Jesus, in a human life. The living Christ in heaven has lived and suffered and died for me on earth. This makes God seem so much nearer. Not only so, but the Holy Spirit, Himself God, indwells my heart by grace and is even now helping me to pray. God is still great but He is also intimately near.

The doctrine is not the creation of theologians, imposed upon rather than derived from Scripture. The object of these studies is to show that the biblical evidence itself demands that we believe in one God, eternally existent in three Persons.

We commence by looking at the evidence for the unity of God. We then consider Old Testament anticipations of the Trinity. After this we look at passages which relate two of the Persons to each other, and finally we consider those passages where the relationship between all Three is presented.

Those who would like to do further study on the doctrine are advised to read the chapter entitled 'The Biblical Doctrine of the Trinity' in 'Biblical Foundations' by B. B. Warfield (Tyndale Press), followed by 'The Doctrine of the Trinity' by L. Hodgson (Nisbet).

THE HOLY TRINITY

The Unity of the Godhead (Pentateuch and History)

1 : 'Hear, O Israel'

Deuteronomy 6.1–19

The Book of Deuteronomy records for us the inspired preaching of Moses at the end of his life. After his death the people of Israel were to move into Canaan and there would find themselves as a free nation settled in a pagan environment. The great purpose of his preaching is to prepare them for that experience.

This chapter contains a section (4–9) which has meant more to the Jew throughout his history than any other passage in the Old Testament. Its opening words, 'Hear, O Israel', mark it out for special attention (cf. Deut. 4.1; 9.1; 20.3; 27.9) and Israel has certainly given it that. It is recited twice every day, along with Deut. 11.13–21 and Num. 15.37–41, by every devout Jew. The Talmud opens with it. Its first great statement represents the nearest to a generally accepted creed that Judaism has ever possessed. It is known as the Shema, from the Hebrew word with which it begins. However we translate its great basic statement (and the RSV text and margin present the various possibilities) it certainly declares that Yahweh (the personal name of God, represented by 'LORD' in the text) and He alone is to be treated as God by His covenant people Israel. An earlier chapter in the same book shows us why: 'the LORD is God; there is no other besides him' (Deut. 4.35, cf. v. 39).

11

This simple statement of faith is followed by a call (echoed in many other parts of Deuteronomy, e.g. 4.29; 10.12; 11.13; 26.16; 30.2, 6, 10) for singlehearted devotion to Him. Indeed, He is a jealous God (14f.), with all the jealousy of holy love for the undivided affection of its beloved. He will not share His throne with any other nor His place in the devotion of His people. When we really love God then we shall want to do His will obediently (1–3, 17f., cf. John 14.15, 21–24; 1 John 5.3) and to train our children in His ways (2, 7).

> 'O how I fear Thee, Living God, with deepest, tenderest fears,
>
> And worship Thee with trembling hope and penitential tears!
>
> Yet I may love Thee, too, O Lord, almighty as Thou art,
>
> For Thou hast stooped to ask of me the love of my poor heart.'

> (Frederick William Faber)

2 : Divine Faithfulness, Human Disloyalty

Deuteronomy 32.1–18

The great Song of Moses (cf. 31.30) is a didactic poem very much after the style of some historical psalms which trace a theme through Israel's history. Moses extols the faithfulness and love of God to a people who returned only rebellion and disloyalty. Their apostasy is set in the context of His fatherly love and care. This is expounded with a wealth of illustrative language—especially in vs. 9–14—which bears the message home to the heart by way of the imagination. Such tender compassion brings into focus the sheer ingratitude of their revolt. As in Deut. 6 God is shown also as a jealous God, that is, concerned for their exclusive devotion (16).

The defection of the Israelites in the wilderness is described in a fourfold way:

1. The gods were 'foreign' (12), 'strange' (16). God had

called His people to separation from other nations and the most important aspect of this was separation from their gods. This was to become a critical issue in the days of Elijah, as we shall see.

2. They were 'gods they had never known' (17, cf. 11.28; 13.6) The Lord had known them and they Him. He had loved them, delivered them from slavery, entered into covenant with them, led them through the wilderness. Now they had forsaken Him for gods who had done nothing for them. The worship of the golden calf (Exod. 32) was at the least a breaking of the second commandment; the worship of Baal-Peor (Num. 25) was a flagrant transgression of the first.

3. They were 'new gods that had come in of late' (17). Modern advertisers overwork the word 'new'. There is one realm at least in which novelty is no virtue but a vice, and that is religion. The Scriptures welcome the new only when it further discloses Him who is eternal.

4. They were 'demons which were no gods' (17, cf Psa. 106.37; 1 Cor. 10.20). Moses does not deny their existence but he does deny their status as gods. This is an important distinction. There is a supernatural world and it is peopled by spiritual beings, but there is One only to whom the great word 'God' can be applied, the one great Creator and Ruler of all.

Jeshurun ('the Upright') is a poetic title for Israel. See Deut. 33.26–29 and Charles Wesley's great hymn (Methodist Hymnbook No. 68).

> 'None is like Jeshurun's God, so great, so strong,
>   so high;
> Lo! He spreads His wings abroad, He rides upon
>   the sky. . . .
> Israel, what hast thou to dread? Safe from all
>   impending harms,
> Round thee and beneath are spread the everlasting
>   arms.'

(Charles Wesley)

3 : The Rock of His People

Deuteronomy 32.19–43

How can we prove that there is one God, and that He is Yahweh, the God of Israel? One Divine argument is worth a thousand from men. The whole thrust of this passage is that the Lord would demonstrate His sole deity by the logic of history. At the end of many centuries the lesson would be clear for all to read.

'They have stirred me to jealousy with what is no god. . . . So I will stir them to jealousy with those who are no people' (21). God shows here how able He is 'to make the punishment fit the crime'. The worship by Israel of alien deities was to be appropriately judged by the sword of alien foes. Some of these foes (for instance, the Assyrians) certainly merited the description 'no people' because of the sheer barbarism of their methods of warfare. God had promised Israel, 'if you walk in my statutes and observe my commandments and do them . . . five of you shall chase a hundred, and a hundred of you shall chase ten thousand; and your enemies shall fall before you by the sword' (Lev. 26.3, 8). This was a striking promise but their flagrant sin against Him would lead God to give their enemies an even more astonishing victory (30).

However could this be construed as an argument for the God of Israel? By the simple fact that 'their rock is not as our Rock' (31). Such an event must have an adequate cause —a supernatural one—and only one adequate supernatural cause existed—the Lord! When it came it would demonstrate not only His omniscience (for this is prediction and not history) but His almighty power.

Would He use His people's enemies to destroy them completely? No, He would bring them to the place of utter helplessness and complete failure of confidence in the false gods (36–38), and then would rise up to deliver them and to show beyond all shadow of doubt His sole Godhead. 'See now that I, even I, am He, and there is no god besides me . . .' (39). The majestic oracles in Isa. 40–48 provide the best commentary on all this.

Prophecy and history together constitute the Lord's own demonstration of His nature. The Bible is the inspired record of both. 'How firm a foundation, ye saints of the Lord, is laid for your faith in His excellent word!'

Meditation: Are there any events in my own life in which the Lord has demonstrated His sole deity?

4 : 'Reign without a rival'

1 Kings 18.17–40

Here is one of the Bible's greatest moments of drama. The situation called for a decisive demonstration of the reality of Yahweh. Ahab not only tolerated the idolatrous worship at Dan and Bethel—all the other kings of the northern kingdom did that—he married the pagan Jezebel of Sidon (1 Kings 16.30-33). She was devoted to the worship of the Tyrian Baal, Melkart, and the people were profoundly influenced by her. God's answer to the situation came through the prophet Elijah. Looking at the matter from the human point of view it might be said that the whole future religious history of Israel was dependent on one man's faith in this moment of crisis.

Ahab did just as Elijah instructed him. This was probably due to fear of the consequences of disobedience. He knew from experience that the prophet was in touch with super-natural power (1 Kings 17.1-7). Asherah was a goddess. Did Elijah remember the ancient word, 'One man of you puts to flight a thousand, since it is the Lord your God who fights for you, as he promised you' (Josh. 23.10)? His calm and confident approach contrasts markedly with the frenzied antics of the pagan prophets as they sought to induce their god to act. This in itself must have impressed the people deeply before ever the miracle of the fire from heaven occurred. Elijah's mocking words (27), charged with the irony which is so often present in the Old Testament but is so often overlooked by the 'wooden' western reader, spurred them on to even greater religious exhibitionism.

Elijah's actions (31–35) showed not only his utter faith in the miraculous power of Yahweh, but his conviction of the unity of all twelve tribes of Israel in a day when the kingdom was divided. He recognized also a continuity with the past (36). The way he named Yahweh as God of the patriarchs was an implicit pleading of the covenant promises. In words

15

which were probably taken from a contemporary proverb, Elijah had challenged the people to decide between Baal and Yahweh (21). It was thus religious syncretism which was the issue. The true God provided His own evidence for the claims being made for Him by His prophet. He always does.

Meditation: If there is only one true God, He can tolerate no rival in the affections of His people.

5 : Mocking the Living God

2 Kings 18.28–19.7

The events described here took place more than one hundred and fifty years after Elijah's contest with the prophets of Baal. The defeat of Jezebel's brand of Baal-worship did not mean the conversion of the mass of Israel's people to true godliness. Indeed, their continued rebelliousness resulted in the fall of Samaria (the capital of the northern kingdom) as a Divine punishment. The instrument of its fall was Assyria (2 Kings 17.1–6). Some years later Sennacherib of Assyria came against Jerusalem, capital of Judah (2 Kings 18.13–17). He sent the Rabshakeh, a high official of the Assyrian Empire, to secure the surrender of the city without the necessity for siege.

Following up his first message to the inhabitants of the city (18.19–25), the Rabshakeh seeks to place all the blame for the city's predicament upon its king and upon his faith in the Lord (29–32). He exalts the king he himself serves (28). The NEB follows the Old Latin version by inserting 'Where are the gods of Samaria' after 'Ivvah' (34). The Assyrian king was regarded as the regent on earth of the god Asshur. Thus, in claiming that he has vanquished the gods of so many of the petty kingdoms of the Fertile Crescent, he is perhaps implying the superiority of his god. This does not excuse his pride, however. Such self-exaltation is everywhere attacked in the Bible and nowhere more so than in Isaiah, whose prophecy also records (in chs. 36, 37) the events given here (cf. Isa. 2.6–22; 14.3–21; etc.).

As Hezekiah (19.4) and Isaiah (19.6) both recognized, clearly this was not to be viewed simply as an attack upon the king but as a deliberate insult to the living God. That last phrase itself was perhaps an expression of Hezekiah's faith. Of course Yahweh could not be treated as if He were on the same level as the gods of Hamath and Sepharvaim! These were nonentities—as was Asshur himself—and just as they had proved completely unable to assist their devotees in time of need, so would the Assyrians find no refuge from the judgement soon to fall upon them.

A thought: 'Pride comes before a fall'—always true, either here or hereafter.

6 : 'Ah, Assyria, the rod of my anger'

2 Kings 19.8–37

The final message of the Rabshakeh (this time in written form) contained nothing new. Hezekiah's prayer recognizes the element of truth in the boastful claim that had been made (17 f.). True prayer is always realistic. It does not mean a shutting of the eyes to things as they are. Joshua and Caleb saw the giants and the walled cities of Canaan just as clearly as the other ten spies (Num. **13, 14**) but towering above all the obstacles to entrance into the land they saw the great God Himself and the promises He had made to His people. Hezekiah was a man of like faith. He too saw the greatness of the Lord (15), and the exploits of the kings of Assyria must have looked very insignificant in comparison. Prayer does not mean that we do not see the same facts; rather, we see them in their true perspective.

Isaiah's prophecy graphically depicts the pride of Sennacherib as seen by God. Contrast Sennacherib's reiterated 'I' (23 f.) with Hezekiah's reiterated 'thou' (15, 19). The proud pagan, both ancient and modern, reckons himself a self-made man, for his paganism has not subdued his pride but only fostered it. The true man of God looks away from himself to Another and glories in what He is and in what He has done. For all his 'perpendicular-personal-pronoun-itis', however, Sennacherib was doing nothing more than execute Divine decrees (25 f.). Isa. **10**.5–19 is the classic passage on this theme. God is the absolute Lord of all

17

history and He uses nations for His purposes, whether they are aware of it or not. It was *not* His purpose that Jerusalem should be taken at this time, however (32–34).

Biblical history contains many ironies. It is certainly striking that the king who had boasted so greatly of his power to overcome nations and cities, despite the 'protection' of their gods, should himself have died at the hand of members of his own family, while engaged in the worship of his own deity! This god (identified by some with Asshur, although there are other possibilities) must be added to the list of impotent deities given in v. 12!

Meditation: 'History is "His story".'

Questions and themes for study and discussion on Studies 1–6

1. The difference between jealousy in God and in man.

2. The use of the language of analogy in application to God (e.g. 'Rock', 'Father'). Are we justified in drawing out *all* the implications of an analogy?

3. The Song of Moses (Deut. 32) is described as 'a witness for me against the people of Israel' (31.19). In what sense?

4. Why was the defeat of Baalism so important in Elijah's day?

5. The expression 'the living God' is found in both the Old and the New Testaments. How does His living power find demonstration today?

6. What Biblical characters besides Sennacherib especially illustrate the pride of the human heart? Why is this so hateful to God?

CHARACTER STUDIES

7 : Elkanah

1 Samuel 1.1–23

The scene is set in the quiet hill-country hamlet of Ramathaim-Zophim. Like Bethlehem it is a backwater of the land, away from the turbulence of the invaders from the eastern desert and the western coastal strip, away too from much of the evil which haunted that century. The chapter might be a continuation of Ruth's story, with the spotlight of the historian changing from the farm of Boaz to the farm of Elkanah.

He was a quiet and somewhat complacent man, this farmer-father of the last of the judges of Israel, an obscure man made great by his son, or perhaps by the devotion of a good wife, whose prayers gave Samuel to his people. Elkanah fulfilled with annual precision the duties of his faith. He made his pilgrimage to the national shrine of Shiloh, where the ark of the covenant was kept, and no doubt felt that by this meticulous observance of the formalities of religion all his duty towards God was done. His was no corrupt worship, nor was his view of God a mean and unworthy one, but there was little of challenge in his faith, nothing to disturb his genial and somewhat shallow complacency.

For observe his household. Elkanah gives no evidence of awareness concerning the division in his house. Doubtless quoting Jacob as his precedent, he supports two wives, and does nothing to quench the venom of the wife who first had children, against her unfortunate partner. Elkanah had no conception of the pain in Hannah's heart, and of the hunger

19

for children of her own, which could not be satisfied by any gifts, by anything, in fact at all, short of the proper fulfilment.

There is a faint touch of the ludicrous in the good man's conviction that the blessing of having him for a husband was in itself compensation. He, surely, he tells the persecuted and distracted woman, is worth more than many sons. And what if Peninnah was harsh to her? Was he not most abundantly kind? He had no word of reproach for Peninnah, who marred a high religious occasion by her waspish attacks on the object of her jealousy. A harmless man, in short, notable for neither good nor ill, but more for good than ill, quietly pleased with himself, and with small concern for the deeper implications of religion.

8 : Peninnah

Proverbs 14.1; 17.1–5

Elkanah's wife Peninnah was an insecure and a tormented woman. The divided household reveals all the evils of anything other than, or short of, holy monogamy. And, as so often happens in life, justice seemed awry. A woman eminently fitted to bring up children, was without offspring. One whose bitter jealousy and hatred unfitted her for the task of motherhood had been entrusted with the rearing of a family.

That this responsibility did not make Peninnah gentle and humble is the measure of that evil which was eating her life away. Of all the passions which afflict man, jealousy is the hardest to bear, exacts the hardest service, and pays the bitterest of wages. It is condemned to watch the success of its enemy. Perhaps Peninnah was younger, less popular with the village, less beautiful than Hannah. Something took away all joy in her children. Merely to see Hannah accepted and high in Elkanah's affections, shallow though those affections were, was gall to her spirit. She was very unsure of her worth, and when the clumsy husband gave his childless wife 'a double portion' at the time of religious festival (1 Sam. 1.5, RV), Peninnah's hatred was stirred to its turbid depths.

Jealousy is the fear or realization of another's superiority, and Peninnah paid her rival this unsolicited compliment, but in entertaining the deadly visitant in her heart, she ruined her peace, and preyed upon herself. Envy, like anger, burns itself in its own fire. It has no other task than that of detracting from another's virtue, and in so doing quenches virtue in its host. As Franklin once remarked: 'Whoever feels pain at hearing of the good of his neighbour will feel a pleasure in the reverse. And those who despair to rise in distinction by their virtues, are happy if others can be depressed to a level with themselves.'

This was Peninnah's fate and her predicament. This was the poison which spoiled the household of Elkanah, without, as far as the evidence of the story goes, any reaction or attention from that self-centred man. The pathetic creature had much to make her contented and happy. Because she could not have more, the first unrivalled place, she destroyed the wealth she had in folly. To some extent she merits pity as the victim of a society which gave woman less than her due.

9 : Hannah

1 Samuel 1.21–2.11

Childlessness was a peculiar burden to a pious Hebrew woman. In such a fate she found herself excluded from the national destiny. ('In thee and in thy seed shall all the families of the earth be blessed' [Gen. **28**.14, AV, KJV]). She could never become the ancestress of the One who should 'bruise the serpent's head'. Hence the peculiar bitterness of the assault Peninnah made upon Hannah's peace. It required a deep grief to attract the attention of Elkanah, but Hannah's distress was such that it brought out all the kindliness of that simply constructed man.

She must have felt that there was no one who truly understood her, and in that conviction is loneliness indeed. It was a further blow when the aged priest, accustomed to the loud and shallow prayers of many of the visitors to his shrine, was too obtuse to mark the distress which sought solitary communion with God for the deep petitions of the heart. The gentleness and moving eloquence of Hannah's reply to his clumsy assessment of her trouble (1.15 f.), is a clear indication of her gentleness of character, and the quiet ways she had learned in the hard school of Peninnah's jealousy and scorn.

Hannah was a woman of undemonstrative faith and deep committal, strong and quietly decisive. She makes up her own mind about visiting the Shiloh festival, and about the career of the child she had been given. Elkanah shows his easy-going acceptance of his wife in a manner which indicates the strength of character he found in her.

The psalm of praise which Hannah sings in Eli's presence (2.1–10) reveals her understanding of divine things in an age when men had small understanding of their God. It recognizes the power of God and the certainty of ultimate justice. It expresses faith in God's power to keep, and joy at answered prayer. It vibrates with gratitude.

Gratitude, this deep characteristic of Hannah's character, is a quality for consideration. Here are some words for consideration: . . . 'A humble mind is the soil out of which thanks naturally grow' (Henry Ward Beecher). . . . 'A thankful heart is not only the greatest virtue, but the parent of all other virtues' (Marcus Tullius Cicero) . . . 'Every virtue divorced from thankfulness is maimed and limps along the spiritual road' (John Henry Jowett) . . . 'O Lord that lends me life, lend me a heart replete with thankfulness' (William Shakespeare).

10 : Hophni and Phinehas

1 Samuel 2.12–36; 4.16–22

Hophni and Phinehas were 'sons of Belial', and the Old Testament has no darker word of reproach. Belial means literally and basically 'worthlessness', and is used of the dissolute, the reprobate and the uncouth. There have been many flashes of history in the story of the judges which illuminate the shocking degradation of the times, but few are more repulsive than that which shows the greed and lechery of the sons of Eli.

There was little enough in this age of divided weakness and infiltrating paganism to unite Israel around the Law and Moses' God, but the shrine of Shiloh, with its sacred memorials of the ancient Tabernacle, was one attempt to attain this end. If corruption found a home and centre there, the damage was grave indeed. In the sons of Eli, the high priest of Shiloh's shrine, it found such a harbourage.

Evil in the two men, who were probably middle-aged, since their father neared the age of ninety, was open, cynical and unconcealed. Nadab and Abihu died because of an act of gross irreverence (Lev. 10). Hophni and Phinehas died also, though less immediately. The ritual for the securing of the priest's portion was established, but roughly disregarded by these uncouth men. Reverence is the first element of religion. It cannot but be felt by anyone who has correct views of the greatness and holiness of God, and of man in relation to God.

Through all time, since the Pharisees and their 'unpardonable sin', their 'blasphemy against the Holy Spirit', of which the Lord accused them, people whose life is lived close to the practice of the forms and rituals of religion have been exposed to the temptation of treating sacred things with levity. Blasphemy lies along that path. The significance of such ministry must be kept with care.

If such unholiness was visible and condoned in the central holy place of Israel, what hope was there for the proper training of the common folk who resorted there in 'the fear of the Lord'? Such was the wider significance of Hophni and Phinehas. Their sin, like all sin, was contagious, but with such carriers at large, what hope was there to contain and to quench the virus? The story is woven with the end of Eli and the beginning of Samuel to reveal the need for the destruction of the old, and the establishment of the new.

11 : Eli

1 Samuel 2.27–36; 4.1–22

Eli sprang, not from the eldest, but the youngest of the sons of Aaron in his descent. Since the older line was passed over in the choice of a priest for Shiloh's shrine, it would appear that once, perhaps in his young manhood, Eli was a person of vigour and devotion.

We meet him only in his old age. In the first chapter of the book he is shown a trifle obtuse and impatient with a case of pathetic need, but rapidly adjusting to the situation when the real facts are courteously put before him. In the second chapter he is shown weakly protesting against the base iniquities of his carnal sons. In the third chapter he is seen in gentle humility receiving from the lips of a child a sombre confirmation of the sentence conveyed to him by 'the man of God'.

There is much therefore about Eli which we do not know. In the few verses which, in these chapters, form the substance of his biography, or at least the later years of it, Eli appears to us a pitiable, a weak, but a pious old man, unable to cope with a mounting wave of evil.

None the less, that evil was of his making. He was passive in days which demanded action, silent in days which called for speech, a weakling in days which cried for strength, and mild when God's name called for passionate defence. He set his family and their concupiscence above the honour of God, and, in his office, there could hardly have been a greater fault.

Verse 30, in the terrible indictment of the unnamed 'man of God', set an immortal verse into the annals of the faith, and put into words a promise which millions have discovered in their life experience to be true, but the same verse, taken in the context of the grim warning, defines and nails down Eli's sin. He had not honoured God. His sons had made themselves vile, and he restrained them not. He was called to exercise discipline, and had failed to exercise it. There was no excuse for his weakness. He stood in high office and the nation mattered more than his family. So Eli died with his last years shadowed by a mistake in his youth or middle age. It was too late.

12 : Temple-boy

1 Samuel 3

It is difficult to estimate the age of Samuel in this story. He must have been old enough to serve as the immediate

24

servant of the aged Eli, strong enough to open the temple doors, and intelligent enough to deliver a detailed message. Shall we say twelve or thirteen years, the age of the Lord in Luke's story of His childhood?

The RSV might have been a little bolder in its translation of the first verse. The NEB puts the situation well: 'Now in those days the word of the Lord was seldom heard.' It was not an unrecognizable situation. Indeed, the whole story could be symbolic. The light in the dim sanctuary was dying down when the Lord spoke to Samuel. A generation had failed but, as John remarked, the darkness does not quench the word, and often when the old have failed He speaks to the young.

But when He does so, He still utters the substance of His own unchanging word. The message comes with new impact, and with new clarity, but Samuel is commissioned to communicate to the erring old man exactly the same penetrating truth as 'the man of God' of the earlier chapter had communicated to him. Truth does not change, but God sometimes finds it necessary to use new voices to carry its message.

The maturity of the boy is evident. He had grown up in the solemn precincts of the shrine of Shiloh, handling divine things, performing, with seeming delight, the divine offices. Hophni and Phinehas had been hardened and brutalized by their careless handling of God's vessels. Familiarity bred contempt. With Samuel the opposite process took place. It depends always with what reverence, and what devotion the work is undertaken. In the case of the little boy, the son of a devout mother, prepared by Hannah's ministrations and prayers for the task of the neophyte, the place of God had been sanctifying.

The story finds its climax in vs. 18 and 19. Samuel delivered the painful message word for word. That is why God confirmed his words. In a day when the faithful failed among the children of men (Psa. **12**.1) Samuel was found to be faithful. We dismiss old Eli with a touch of sorrow. To hear his doom from a child he loved must have been pain indeed.

13 : Samuel the Judge

1 Samuel 7

Samuel was a judge in a wider sense of the word than any of his predecessors, who in general were men brought forward by some national crisis, and inspired to some act of patriotic deliverance. Verse 16 shows Samuel on circuit, dispensing justice in local courts, and in the act giving some unity to the perilously divided tribes. It was something of the same task as Henry II undertook for England in the Middle Ages.

Samuel's policy of unification was needed now that the sketchy cohesion which had made Shiloh its centre had been destroyed. The deep Philistine raiding, in which the house of Eli had perished, also overran Shiloh. The chronicler of Samuel does not mention this. The raid, the looting and the murder of the priests are mentioned by the psalmist (**78**.60–64) and Jeremiah (**7**.12; **26**.9). The grim experience, and the escape from the raiders, may have been traumatic for the young boy who served the shrine. So, too, may have been the loss of that sacred talisman the Ark.

Had Shiloh stood, Samuel might have been tempted to follow the tradition of Eli, and function rather as pontiff than legislator. It was a legislator, rather than a high priest, which the situation in the land demanded, and the pressure of circumstances forced the role on Samuel. This is what faith should seek in life—a proper function in relation to events, and the meaning of those situations in which God places us or allows us to be placed. It is thus that He guides a mind alert to discover His will. Shiloh, and the priesthood associated with it, had seen their day.

Samuel, from the wealth of his experience, struck a more spiritual note than any other leader had done since Joshua. Observe the tenor of his address to assembled Israel. The old monotheistic tradition, with its rejection of idolatry, was not dead. It needed a voice, and Samuel gave it one. The people responded with vigour, as the reaction to the Philistine raid shows. It is a testimony to Samuel's leadership. He was no soldier, but he supplied what no soldier dare lack—a rank and file filled with belief in their cause.

14 : Samuel's Sons

1 Samuel 8.1–6; Deuteronomy 4.9, 10; 11.18–21

With all the shocking example of Eli before him Samuel failed to hold his children. He himself had set them no example of corruption or of unfairness. And yet the young men, Joel and Abijah, who held court on their father's behalf on the edge of the southern desert, became notorious for the taking of bribes and the perversion of justice.

How is this to be accounted for? Let it be stated immediately that it is not always the fault of parents if their children do not follow in their steps. At the same time, if visited by such a calamity, parents should search their life, their attitudes, their outlook, in earnest endeavour to discover, if possible, the cause of failure, and to put it right.

Wherein could a good man like Samuel have failed so lamentably? Perhaps he was too much absent from home, busy on the tasks of his national leadership. Perhaps, following the advice which Jethro gave once to Moses, he should have acquired the art of delegation, and brought again to life Moses' effective scheme of co-operative justice. Perhaps Samuel was too eager to hold the reins of power in his own hands, and, inevitably overworked, had not found time for that fellowship with his family which is such a vital element in the upbringing of the young. There are times when boys need their father, as a guide, a confidant and a friend. It is a primary duty for a father, and the successful leading of one's children to God must be a priority in all of life's activities.

Perhaps, in spite of the sombre warning of Eli's example, Samuel had been too eager to see his sons follow in his steps as legislators. No mistake produces such unfortunate results as misguided parental efforts to force children into a predetermined pattern of life. Parental ambitions do not matter. What does matter is that young men and women should find the career for which they are fitted and in which they can find true fulfilment and happiness. When Mark clashed with Paul, the fault may perhaps be traced to the desire of Mary his mother, or his uncle Barnabas, to see the young man take up a missionary career. His role was to write a Gospel, Joel and Abijah were not fitted to hold a judicial role, and it was a disservice to them and to Israel to thrust them into such a position.

This is guesswork, but it is obvious that, in upbringing or in premature and unwise appointment, somewhere along the line of life, Samuel had failed.

15 : Samuel's Crisis

1 Samuel 8

Samuel took the demand for a king as a vote of no confidence. The fact confirms the suspicion that a basic fault in him was a certain infusion of pride. He was old. His sons had betrayed him. No one else was trained to succeed him. He had made no provision for the continuation of the magnificent work he had done save the unwise and abortive attempt to found a line of judges. This was a quite lamentable lack, and betokened a reprehensible measure of self-esteem.

In the united demand for the establishment of a monarchy, there was some indication of the effectiveness of Samuel's work. Here, after all, was Israel speaking with a united voice, and this unity was, without a doubt, a product of Samuel's judgeship, and his establishment of a system of justice. Had he, by the acceptable choice of a successor, in the way in which Moses chose Joshua, or alternatively, had he, in a wise system of delegation, after the same Mosaic pattern, left a framework of judicial power in the land, the demand for a monarchy might never have arisen. Samuel must be blamed for some of it.

Perhaps then, as we have remarked, a corner of Samuel's basic pride is seen when he takes the demand of the people as a rejection of himself. The people, in fact, had been notably patient. The leader was old. His sons were unsuitable to succeed him. It was becoming late, and many could remember the near-anarchy of the years before Samuel took power in the land. It is then pointed out to Samuel that it was not the judge who was rejected, but rather God Himself. The ideal constitution for Israel was a theocracy, with power administered through the priests. Failing this, a guided monarchy was the next best plan. This becomes clear to

Samuel, and it became clear because of his unbroken habit
of seeking God's will, and faithfully telling the people what
he had learned in the holy place of such communion. His
experience as a child in the Temple set the pattern for old
age. Life is not infrequently so ordained. Without reserve or
trimming of words, the old judge explains the financial and
religious implications of their demand. The people were un-
convinced.

Questions and themes for study and discussion on Studies 7–15

1. What are the roots of jealousy? Consider Sarah, Rachel
   and Leah, and Joseph's brothers.

2. What is irreverence?

3. What is blasphemy?

4. How can parents best ensure their children's loyalty to
   their own ideals?

5. Why do some characters find delegation difficult?

THE HOLY TRINITY

The Unity of the Godhead (Psalms, Prophets, and New Testament)

16 : Universal Worship

Psalm 86

It is sometimes maintained that true monotheism was attained only in the later stages of Israel's history (notably in the prophecies of Isa. **40–66**), and that much of the Old Testament is the product of men who were monolatrous or henotheistic in outlook. Monolatry or henotheism is the idea that many gods exist but that I am to worship and serve one alone, for he is *my* god. In support of this claim it is often pointed out that the writers of the Old Testament sometimes write of other gods as if they possess objective existence.

Our present passage enables us to see that this does not necessarily mean that they exist *as gods* (cf. Deut. **32**.16 f.). Although on its own v. 8 *could* support such an idea, v. 10 shows that such an inference would have been quite mistaken. In such passages then, the word 'god' identifies the being in terms of the valuation placed upon him by his worshippers. Although he may be a supernatural being (a demon), however, there is only one true God.

This psalm was written by a man in some obvious distress, and conscious of opposition from evil men (14, 17). The psalmist does not, however, indulge in self-pity or give way to excessive occupation with his plight. Rather, he looks outward and upward to God. He reflects on the nature and works of God (5, 8, 10, 13, 15), and this causes him to cast himself upon Him. This is the way for the servants of God still. We need to take the great biblical affirmations about the power, character and gracious works of God, and dwell upon them. This is how faith grows and how assurance comes in the midst of tribulation.

It is because God is great and because He has done such great things, that the psalmist is so convinced that all men must ultimately come to acknowledge Him in worship (8–10). The psalmist knew very well that 'all the nations' were worshippers of false gods but he knew that the Lord's supremacy must be universally accepted in due time. In the New Testament we see clearly that this is effected through the Lord Jesus Christ (Phil. 2.9–11).

> 'O the joy to see Thee reigning, Thee, my own beloved Lord!
> Every tongue Thy name confessing, worship, honour, glory, blessing
> Brought to Thee with glad accord—
> Thee, my Master and my Friend, vindicated and enthroned,
> Unto earth's remotest end glorified, adored, and owned.'

> (Frances Ridley Havergal)

17 : 'The Lord reigns'

Psalm 97

Psalms 93, 97 and 99 all open with the great affirmation 'the Lord reigns', and each of these psalms draws out some of the implications of this statement. The doctrinal basis of the Inter-Varsity Fellowship affirms belief in 'the sovereignty of God in creation, revelation, redemption and final judgement.' This is fundamental to the very idea of God. If He is not supreme then what does the word 'God' mean? Psalm 93 lays emphasis upon the fact that He reigns in majesty, Psalm 99 that He reigns in holiness, and Psalm 97 that He reigns in righteousness.

A strongly ethical note is therefore sounded in Psa. 97.

31

There is here something of that moral awesomeness which characterized the giving of the Law at Sinai and the revelation of God to Isaiah in the Temple at Jerusalem. If there is one God and He is supreme, then it is of great importance that we should know what He is like. History contains many examples of the misuse of power by men of bad character. The greater the power the more important it is that it is in the hands of a person of righteousness and integrity. It is a source of infinite comfort that the only Being who has all power is utterly righteous and just.

The word 'righteousness' may sound rather a cold one to the modern reader but there is no lack of warmth in this psalm. It is characterized by joy and gladness (1, 8, 11 f.) Paganism is so utterly joyless. The animist and the polytheist are deeply conscious of the conflict of spirits and deities and feel themselves to be in the centre of a struggle between beings greater and more powerful than themselves. To be brought out of this situation into one where one great and righteous God is in ultimate control of all that happens and calls us His own people, floods the heart with joy. Notice the strong expression of v. 9, 'far above' (cf. Eph. 1.21) The great and true God is on a different plane altogether from the false deities men worship.

A Thought : The affirmation of His sole deity cuts all other supernatural beings down to size.

18 : The Folly of Idolatry

Isaiah 44.6–20

From ch. 40 onwards the prophecies of Isaiah are directed towards a people who could look back on the overthrow of Jerusalem by the Babylonians as a fact of history. They were living in exile in Babylon and therefore in the midst of a polytheistic people. This accounts for the strong attack on idolatry which occur in chs. 40–48. Yahweh is the God of Israel, for she is the covenant people, and yet at the same time, as the First and the Last, He is the Lord of all human history (6, cf. Rev. 1.17; 2.8; 22.13).

One of the chief evidences of His sole deity is His power

to predict the future through His prophets (7 f.). The unfolding story of the Bible is very largely a story of promise and fulfilment, and the predictive element in the Old Testament is very strong indeed. The fulfilment of prophecy bears eloquent testimony to Him from whom it proceeded. This sets Him apart from the gods of paganism.

Verses 9–20 are a scathing attack on the folly of idolatry. The prophet ridicules the whole project of idol-making. It does indeed furnish an illustration of the effect of sin upon the mind. There is nothing more fundamentally illogical than sin. The sinner knows in his own heart that he cannot sin with impunity or escape the consequences of his sin indefinitely—and yet he goes on sinning! The devil is well aware of the superior power of the God against whom he is in rebellion —and yet he does not give up the contest. The construction and worship of idols does not bear a moment's investigation in the light of reason, let alone revelation. The biblical revelation is addressed to faith, but, once faith is established, the believer discovers that his reason also is deeply satisfied by all that God reveals about Himself and His wonderful ways with the sons of men.

Meditation: To know and worship the true God is to come to a new understanding of everything.

19 : Carrying or Carried?

Isaiah 46

The Persian conqueror has entered Babylon. Its gods have been unable to protect it from him. Bel is identical with Marduk, Babylon's chief deity, and Nebo was his son. They are to be found in such compound names as Belshazzar and Nebuchadnezzar. No doubt images of these gods had often been carried with great pomp in ceremonial processions through the streets of the city. Now, their impotence for ever established, they are loaded on to beasts of burden and carried away as part of the conqueror's spoils of victory (1 f.).

The God of Israel calls the attention of His people to the great contrast between these idols and Himself (3 f.). The word 'I' occurs with emphasis five times over in the Hebrew of v. 4. Throughout their history, ever since He brought them forth at the Exodus (or possibly in the call of Abraham, **51.**1 f.), God had acted as a mother to them (cf. Deut. **32.**10 ff.). Human parents look after their children only until they are old enough to move off and fend for themselves. Eventually the parents die. But God never ceases to act the full role of Parent to His people. The gods of Babylon could not even save their worshippers in the moment of supreme crisis; the God of Israel carries His people every moment of every day.

This section of Isaiah is full of great rhetorical questions (5, cf. **40.**12–14, 18, 21, 25, 27 f.; **41.**2, 4, 26; **42.**19, 23 f.; **43.**19; **44.**7 f., etc.) The most frequent note sounded in these questions is the invitation to find someone to whom the Lord may be compared. Moreover, comparison perhaps implies idolatry, for an idol provides a visible basis for comparison. The God of Israel, however, is a spiritual Being and One who acts for His people (8–13). The idol is confined to one place by the very fact of its material form and this is a fit symbol of its impotence (6 f.). The people of Israel had experienced the mercy and the judgement of God in the land of Canaan and were now in Babylon. He was just as truly present with them there as He has been in their homeland. He was no merely parochial deity, presiding like some of the Baals over a patch of ground or like Bel over the fortunes of a whole nation. He was the God of heaven and earth, the sole Monarch of the universe (9).

A Thought : Verses 3 f. refer to the nation of Israel but the Christian may take them to himself, for they fitly express God's relationship to him also.

20 : Important Questions

Mark 12.28–37

People begin to ask questions almost as soon as they learn to speak. Some of these are trivial, others of greater importance. The most important concern the spiritual realm, and the deepest of all are about God. Our Lord answered many questions on the great day of questions, a short while before

His death (Mark 11.27—12.34), but the most important was the final one, because it concerned God and man's relationship with Him.

Christ's answer revealed clearly His own acceptance of the rabbinic conviction of the special importance of the Shema (cf. Study No. 1), His teaching that love is the fulfilment of the Law both in relation to God and in relation to man, and His unqualified acceptance of the monotheism of the Old Testament. Nowhere in His teaching does He attack this but always takes the unity of the Godhead for granted (John 5.44; 17.3). Jews and Moslems sometimes misunderstand the Christian doctrine of the Trinity and imagine the New Testament to teach that there are three gods. This is far from the truth.

Of greater importance even than the questions which men ask of God are the questions which God asks of men. The day of questions ended with a great question put by Jesus to His hearers (35–37). The question and His own implied answer show us clearly that His acceptance of God's unity did not rule out a personal claim to deity. His understanding of Psa. 110 shows His complete rejection of the rabbinic notion of a purely human Messiah. The extent to which this psalm is employed in the New Testament (and it is quoted or echoed more often than any other Old Testament passage of comparable length) shows how deeply impressed the men of the New Testament were by our Lord's own interpretation of it.

In this section of our studies we are concerned with the unity of God. As soon as we move into the New Testament, however, we find that we cannot evade the claim of Jesus to be a Divine Person. So the mind is compelled to think and the heart to worship.

21 : 'One God . . . and one Lord

1 Corinthians 8

Much of 1 Corinthians is concerned with questions put to the apostle Paul by the Corinthian Christians. This is true of the present chapter (1, cf. 7.1). It was quite impossible to live in a city like Corinth without encountering meat offered to idols and it was not always possible to tell whether it had been so offered or not. This obviously constituted a problem for Christians, and it is evident from this chapter that there were different approaches to it among the Corinthian believers.

The words placed in quotation marks in the RSV (1, 4) are probably quotations from their letter to Paul. The two quoted statements in v. 4 are of course related to each other. If there is only one God, then it follows that an idol has no real existence in the sense that it does not really represent what it is intended to symbolize—a divine being. As we have seen in earlier studies, this is certainly the position of the Old Testament. Paul clearly held this position himself—although he did not accept all the inferences some of the Corinthians drew from it.

The Christian position (5 f.) is that there is one God and one Lord. The terms 'god' and 'lord' were widely used, of course, in the pagan world of Paul's day and were closely related. If there was a distinction, the former belonged to the language of theology or philosophy and the latter to that of worship and service. They were applied to the same beings, however. The paradox of the Christian position appears here. Paul is asserting in categorical terms the oneness of *God* and yet he affirms also that there is one *Lord* and that He is Jesus Christ! He suggests only one distinction: the Father is the Author of creation and the Son the Agent of it. We will explore this distinction more fully later.

'However, not all possess this knowledge.' What does he mean? Can a man be a Christian and not a monotheist? No, but the simple believer may not have seen all the implications of his monotheism. Indeed, has any believer plumbed the depths of that simple statement 'there is no God but one'?

Questions and themes for study and discussion on Studies 16–21

1. Consider the devotional importance of dwelling upon the nature and the works of God.

2. The basic biblical doctrine of God is often described as 'ethical monotheism.' Why is it important to stress the adjective as well as the noun?

3. Is it right to describe faith as irrational?

4. Do Isa. 44.6–20 and Isa. 46 justify the use of ridicule in evangelism? Was the prophet an evangelist in the usual sense of the term?

5. Why did Jesus say to the scribe, 'You are not far from the kingdom of God' (Mark 12.34)?

6. Are there any ways in which I act as if there was more than one deity?

CHARACTER STUDIES

22 : Saul

1 Samuel 9 and 10

Saul is not unlike the 'rich young ruler' who brought his
shallow enthusiasm to Christ. He had much, but lacked the
essential surrender to God. Saul appears in the ninth chapter
in a humble role, the dutiful son of a rich family wandering
the highlands of central Palestine in search of some valuable
animals.

He must be pictured, therefore, as a man of some self-
reliance and courage. It was no land, in those days, to wander
through with impunity. Saul had a servant with him, who
must be added to the list of faithful henchmen whom we
have met, from Eliezer of Damascus to the servant of
Gideon. Saul had a way with men, a gift of true leadership,
and the servant moves confidently by the side of his stalwart
young master, as much a friend and a counsellor as an
underling.

There is much therefore to commend the man in whom old
Samuel found the future king of Israel. The aged judge saw in
the remarkable sequence of circumstances, which brought the
son of Kish to the meeting place, a situation so unusual that
he found in it the hand of God. Saul obviously had the
physique and the presence which would commend him to
the people who looked for a leader among the nations, a
popular figure fitted to unite scattered and suspicious tribes
round some symbol of unity. It is in mind and spirit that he
lacked something.

Yet the hesitation which he shows in the face of Samuel's
astonishing announcement is no mark against him. It is a

becoming diffidence, a true humility. It was necessary for Samuel to talk long and earnestly to him, in unrecorded conversation, to convince the man of Benjamin that there was a genuine call to him to take up the burden of leadership and overcome reluctance.

How deeply Samuel influenced him is not clear. The tenth chapter shows Saul's need for confirmatory signs. Saul has what seems to have been a deep religious experience with a group of religious celebrants, but it is to be doubted whether he ever attained a rich, meaningful and sustaining faith. Prophets to him were 'seers', men of divine magic, and God a somewhat blurred idea. Hence the failure to carry the full approval of the land. He failed to win 'the worthless' (10.27), but accepted their scorn in humble silence. We feel a shadow upon Saul, and can understand how Samuel yearned over him.

23 : Saul the Soldier

1 Samuel 11

Saul went back to his daily tasks. His call had come, but not his moment. It was a month later, according to Josephus, that Israel was stirred by shocking news. The remnants of the nation who had chosen to remain to the east of Jordan had as their reward the well-watered uplands and valley pastures of Gilead, but at the price of some grave disadvantages. They were exposed to the people of the desert, and the tribes who, like the Ammonites, cultivated the desert edge.

Still remembering their old humiliation under Jephthah, the people of Ammon, strong and arrogant again, came in array against Jabesh and offered the unhappy Gileadites, as the price of peace, mutilation and sadistic humiliation. Messengers hurried through Israel, and it is a sign of the new unity that Samuel's judgeship had achieved, that a wave of horror and indignation went through the land. Saul saw that his hour was come. In many ways it was his finest hour, for shadows were to fall early across his reign. At this moment he shows himself decisive, ardent, a true leader of men, and wise enough to seize an occasion of national stress and unity to show his worth, and rally the people behind him.

Riding this wave of pity and concern for their sundered brethren across the Jordan, Saul collected his army and marched. It must have been forced and exhausting marching. David, in retreat from Absalom, seems to have taken three days to accomplish a comparable march. How long Saul took is not clear, though he appears to have promised a decisive intervention within twenty-four hours of the messengers' reporting back.

Such was the dynamism of his leadership that he did precisely this. It was no easy march from the central uplands of Israel down into the jungle tangle of the Jordan Rift Valley ('the swellings of Jordan' of the AV [KJV] phrase), up the trans-Jordan mountain slopes, and to Jabesh. Without pausing for breath, and achieving surprise by the threefold division of his forces, Saul fell upon the cruel invaders, and won a spectacular victory. The men of Jabesh never forgot it (1 Sam. 31.11).

The effect on Israel was equally spectacular. The tribes had their hero (12). On the surge of sudden and unifying popularity, Saul became the accepted monarch. It was a time of universal rejoicing, a sort of V Day (15). Saul is shown at his best (13). Perhaps he might always have been like this had he known God better. And was that lack partly Samuel's fault?

24 : Samuel's Testimony

1 Samuel 12; Job 8.8–10

Samuel appears to have been the only one of the judges who was deeply conscious of his nation's history. Perhaps his childhood as the temple-servant at Shiloh had given him access to the stored records of the past. Such records there certainly were, and where would they have been more appropriately housed than in the place where Israel's holy relics were kept?

At any rate, he shows in this encounter with the people a very wide knowledge of Israel's history and its significance. His whole approach, his speed of almost defiant challenge, his tone of authority and command are modelled on Joshua's last words. His rapid survey of history from the Exodus, on through the troubled story of the nation to Samson and the day of Saul's victory, shows a sense of the nation's destiny long lacking in the stormy characters who were called to her leadership.

The appeal to experience, and the endeavour to root the nation's faith in the realization of God's active hand in their affairs, was a sound and constant preoccupation with Samuel. He had struck that note when he set up the stone called Ebenezer, between Mizpah and Jeshanah [Shen] (1 Sam. 7.12). The word means: 'Stone of Help'—help, that is, from God. Furthermore, Samuel was prompted to the symbolic action by his own knowledge of history. Mizpah, the name of the Benjamite town (Josh. **18**.26), means 'watchtower', and had perhaps reminded the judge that this was a name which Jacob had given to a cairn set up as a memorial of the agreement between him and Laban (Gen. **31**.45–49). It was a significant memorial. 'Not to know what was done in former times,' said Cicero, 'is to be always a child. If no use is made of the toil and trouble of past ages, the world must remain for ever in the infancy of knowledge.'

Words of counsel could hardly be nobler than those which Samuel uttered before the assembled multitudes as the conclusion of his speech (20–24). Here was Israel's religion in brief, as Moses and Joshua might have put it. The worth of history is shown in the words. A nation loses contact with its past to its dire peril—a point to be considered by those who order education, or preach the message of the Christian faith—an historically grounded religion.

25 : Saul's Impatience

1 Samuel 13

Saul faced a grave military crisis at the end of the second year of his reign. The Philistines were on the march again, and Saul was finding it difficult to hold the people to their newly discovered unity. The threat, too, was grave, and the people followed Saul's leadership with much misgiving. The mood of confidence was gone (7).

It was at this point that Samuel, whose religious prestige was tremendous in the land, chose to delay his coming. Whereupon, as the heading in one popular reference Bible puts it, Saul 'intruded into the priests' office', and offered a sacrifice. It is difficult to be censorious over this act of haste. Saul saw the need for despatch. The army was melting away. Perhaps he should have remembered Gideon, but it was the business of Samuel, if he guarded jealously, as was just, the office of priest, to be at Gilgal in order to bring such significant history to Saul's and the people's remembrance.

Saul, as we have seen, had no deep spirituality. The sacrifice was a formality, and it is here perhaps that some truth and justice must be accorded the rebuke which Samuel gave.

It was not so much the 'intrusion into the priest's office' which condemned Saul's reign to failure or to inconclusiveness, but the impatience with delay, born of an inadequate view of his God, which prompted a perfunctory act of sacrifice.

It is probably quite true that Saul undertook the task of sacrifice with some reluctance (12), but apparently he had received a clear direction regarding the limitations of his royal prerogatives (13), and deliberately disobeyed them. Here was the weakness which was to prove disastrous.

The task of conflict, none the less, was faced with courage. The situation was interesting historically, for here, in a clear record, was the Bronze Age encountering the Iron Age (19–23). The weapon-gap could be closed only by faith, and the confidence and ardour which arise from utter dedication to a cause. This had been shown in the Jabesh-Gilead campaign. Saul could not see the same Spirit abroad when he faced the Philistines. But Saul had one immense and unappreciated advantage—a soldier for a son.

26 : Jonathan

1 Samuel 14.1–15

Jonathan is one of the great characters of the Old Testament, brave, loyal, gracious, a soldier and a friend. The story of his exploit at Michmash reveals much of his person. He was the stuff of which commandoes are made. He could inspire the absolute and unquestioning loyalty of his cool young armourbearer, worthily the theme of a Moody and Sankey hymn. He was simple in his faith and ready to act on it.

The details of Jonathan's manoeuvre are not clear. The Philistines held a commanding hill-position, but clearly one which could be turned, and itself outflanked by a force able to climb unseen and unopposed up a steep ascent. It is fairly obvious from accounts of Philistine reactions in earlier chapters that, as a people, they were prone to panic. This was the flaw of character that Jonathan was determined to turn to his advantage.

Suddenly the Philistine garrison on the hilltop saw two Hebrew warriors, in iron armour like their own, appear over the skyline above them, Jonathan may have been able to give the impression that an effective force was on the way up behind him. At the sight, the garrison on the plateau fled in panic. Their way of retreat was probably a narrow hill-path, so that the panic-stricken soldiers thrust one another to their deaths in their haste to reach safety. It was a piece of astounding bluff, which gave the prince his victory, but it required a courageous and a resourceful man to stage it.

Lest the situation appear unlikely, there is comparatively modern confirmation. A battalion of Allenby's London Regiment in 1917 was located where Saul held his six hundred on that occasion. The local place-name of Mukmas prompted the commander to read his Old Testament. He concluded that the Turks who barred his path were positioned like the Philistines. Reconnaissance showed that the lay of the land had not changed, and that the Turkish position could be turned after the ancient model. A platoon was sent out to occupy the superior position, and when dawn revealed their presence, the Turkish garrison withdrew.

So Jonathan, ill-starred and shadowed by his passionate father, enters the story. He is not destined to stay in it long, or to play the part he might, in happier circumstances, have played, but he is good to know.

27 : Saul and his Son

1 Samuel 14.16–46

On the heights of Michmash, Jonathan had the Philistines
in flight. The distant noise roused Saul. In his excitement (19)
he waved aside the priest. He was too busy to pray. It was
the same impatience he had shown before (13.8–10). In his
pagan folly he condemned his army to hunger. Consider the
results. The victory was incomplete. In the evening the
desperate people broke the law (32). Now, at last, Saul
thought to pray, or to perform that mechanical ritual to
which he reduced such an exercise. Like many who pray only
at such times, and in such perfunctory fashion, he felt cold,
rejected and unheard (37). Too unspiritual and obtuse to
apprehend the true cause in himself and his sin, Saul remembered his foolish vow . . . God sometimes allows folly to
work itself out. He allowed Jonathan to stand incongruously
condemned. And Saul would actually have killed Jonathan!
A surge of anger through the Hebrew host was all that saved
the splendid young warrior. And so Saul, scrupulous of
superstition, and so careless of obedience, blunders on to
Endor. The chapter is rich in lessons, and the spoiling faults
of Saul's character emerge again . . .

The contrast between Saul and his son is striking. Saul
was a hot-headed and passionate man. This side of his
character, properly ordered and controlled, might have led
him far. It determined the ardour of his drive against the
Ammonites before Jabesh-Gilead. But Saul never broke
through to a lofty and dominating faith. God to him was
an elemental power to be propitiated, or appeased and
harnessed by some movements of formality. Jonathan, on
the other hand, was as cool-headed as he was brave. He
could assess his father's folly (29), and probably undertook his
lonely exploit because he had no confidence in winning the
jealous Saul's sanction. Had he been spared his sad ending he
would have made a splendid king, but it is part of the tragedy
of Saul that he dragged to ruin his fine son. Such involve-
ment is inseparable from our humanity. The same basic
fact worked through to tragedy in Achan's family (Jos. 7).
The same truth can be rich and fruitful in joy.

28 : Saul and Samuel

1 Samuel 15

The modern world, weary of war and bloodshed, may find this chapter, with Samuel's decree of destruction against the Amalekites, disturbing to read. The Amalekites must first be seen for what they were—a species of Bedouin tribe, ranging the eastern borderlands of Israel from Sinai and the Arabah northwards, harassing the frontier, raiding, looting, murdering. If peace was to reign in Palestine, their utter defeat was necessary. The war must be seen in the context of war such as this century has known, where beleagured nations have had cruelty, aggression and the determination of desperate guerrilla groups cursing their borderlands and damaging all peace. Saul had a task such as the Emperor Augustus had at the beginning of this era—the pacification of the frontiers behind which peace and prosperity were to grow. For a ruler of Israel it was a national duty.

So much for the task. Speaking of the corruption and utter decadence of the pagan tribes of Canaan, one archaeologist has remarked that, to him, the wonder was not that a sentence of elimination went out against such damaged stocks, but that it was delayed so long. At any rate Saul had his orders. He knew the facts which Ezra was to stress (Ezra 9.11). And Saul, as was his way, interpreted those orders as he saw fit. It was not in mercy that he spared Agag, the sadistic ruler of the desert tribes (33), but for some personal satisfaction, a species of triumphal procession perhaps, with the captive king walking before his chariot. It was an act of royal pride.

He lied to Samuel. He blamed 'the people' (21) for what he had himself sanctioned. He demonstrated once more, and this time for the last time, his untrustworthiness. His was to be no continuing monarchy. Such self-will contained the seeds of its own final defeat. Samuel knew it, and grieved for Saul (35), for he had loved the man whom his own hands had anointed. He saw his face no more.

Samuel in his stern rebuke shows himself the forerunner of the major prophets. His remark about obedience and sacrifice (22) should be read in connection with the first call of Isaiah to Israel (Isa. 1.11–20), three centuries later. It was the old lesson which Israel found it so difficult to learn.

45

Read Psa. **119** and observe the dominance of the theme of obedience.

Questions and themes for study and discussion on Studies 22–28

1. Was Saul a wrong choice?
2. What is popularity worth?
3. Saul's view of God.
4. The centrality of obedience in religion.
5. The purpose of waiting, and the folly of impatience.

THE HOLY TRINITY

Old Testament Anticipations of the Trinity
(History and Poetry)

29 : God Speaks in the Plural

Genesis 1.26–27; 11.1–9

We commence today a series of readings on Old Testament anticipations of the doctrine of the Trinity. We must remember that this doctrine was revealed historically. It was not fully made known until the Incarnation and Pentecost had given men a fuller understanding of the Son and the Spirit, and their relation to each other and to the Father. We should not therefore expect to find the doctrine in its full form in the Old Testament. We should not be surprised, however, to find that the earlier revelation contained anticipations of the later.

The first person plural of Gen. 1.26; 11.7 has often been regarded as such an anticipation (cf. also 3.22), and as needing the doctrine of the Trinity to explain it. Some consider, on the other hand, that 'the explanation of the first person plural forms is probably that the Creator speaks as heaven's King accompanied by His heavenly hosts' (M. G. Kline). We probably cannot be too dogmatic as to the Trinitarian interpretation but if it is correct it has some interesting implications in both passages.

The creation story tells us that when God created man in His own image 'male and female created he them' (1.27). Perhaps this suggests that man in community more fully reflects the Divine image than man in isolation, for God is

Himself a holy Community of Persons. We must be careful how we handle this idea, however; those Christians from whom Mohammed gained his knowledge of Christianity left him with the impression that the Trinity was a Divine community of Father, Mother and Child! In ch. 11, God mockingly impersonates the language of men with His 'Come, let us go down' (7, cf. 3f.). These men were a rebellious community set upon an evil purpose. God is a holy Community set upon a holy purpose.

Meditation: Does my relationship with those nearest to me reflect adequately the image of the true God?

30 : The Angel of the Lord

Genesis 16.7–15; 48.8–16

Angels are normally treated in Scripture as being created by God and altogether inferior to Him; His servants sent to perform His will. This is not true, however, of the Being referred to in the Old Testament as 'the Angel of the Lord'. He is clearly in some sense a separate Person from God, and yet He speaks as if He is God (Gen. 21.17–19; 22. 11 f.; 31.11–13; Judg. 6.11–24; 13.21 f., etc.) The very first occurrence of this phenomenon is in Gen. 16.7–15. It should be noted that the identification of the angel of the Lord with the Lord Himself is not simply Hagar's own. If this had been so she might have been mistaken. The inspired writer also makes this identification (13).

It seems that we are intended to understand the angel of the Lord as a manifestation of the Lord Himself. If God could manifest Himself in fullness in the total life and character of Jesus Christ, then this present phenomenon should present us with no great problem. 'Whenever he is mentioned, he immediately takes his place at the centre of the event' (Von Rad). The same was to be true of Jesus.

Gen. 48.8–16 records an event towards the close of Jacob's life. Here he is virtually adopting Joseph's two sons as his own, so making them tribal heads like their uncles. He alters the order of them, as God had done with Esau and himself and with Isaac and Ishmael. The threefold character of the reference to the One from whom the blessing would come is worth noting, and also the identification of God with 'the angel who has redeemed me from all evil' (15 f.). The verb 'bless' is in the singular. The word 'angel' may well have been suggested by the story of Peniel (Gen. 32.22–32), and the sense that Jacob had, that the man who wrestled with him that night was none other than the Angel of the Lord and so was a manifestation of God Himself. Hos. 12.3 f. also appears to identify God and the angel in the Peniel story.

A thought: Jacob had some striking encounters with God, but he saw Him not only in these but in the whole course of life. Do I?

31 : The Triune Name

Numbers 6.22–27; Matthew 28.16–20

The function of the priest in Israel was mainly sacrificial but he did have other duties also. In Lev. 9.22 f. we see Aaron blessing the people after offering sacrifice on their behalf. His blessing would convey to them the fact that their sacrifice had been accepted by the God he represented.

In Num. 6.22–27 the wording of the priestly blessing is given and it assumes a threefold pattern. In its beautiful phraseology we may see a possible background to the words of blessing found in the greeting at the commencement of many of the New Testament epistles, i.e. 'grace . . . and peace' (Rom. 1.7; 1 Cor. 1.3; 1 Thess. 1.1; Tit. 1.4; 1 Pet. 1.2; Rev. 1.4, etc.), 'grace, mercy and peace' (1 Tim. 1.2; 2 John 3, etc.) and 'mercy, peace and love' (Jude 2). We notice that some of these take a threefold form.

In so blessing the people the priest is said to put God's name on them (27). We find this association of God's blessing with His name also in Deut. 28.9 f. God blesses those who are called by His name (Dan. 9.19, cf. 1 Cor. 6.11). It is He who has chosen to give his people his Name. He is like a father whose children bear his name and receive his blessing. All this gains significance immensely when we realize that for the Hebrew somehow the name was regarded as an expression of what the person was. When God was going to change a man He sometimes changed his name first of all as a pledge of His future work in him (Gen. 25.26; 32.27–30). Gen. 32 shows God changing Jacob's name but also it reveals Jacob asking God what His name is. If Israel are to bear His name then they are to reveal His nature, His character.

This use of the term 'name' in connection with a threefold formula of blessing throws light on Matt. 28.16–20. There, after His resurrection from the dead, our Lord commissioned His disciples to spread the gospel and gave them the baptismal formula. It is not impossible that there was an association between this and Num. 6 in His own mind. This formula excludes a number of heresies. It excludes tritheism (belief in three gods), unitarianism (that form of monotheism which allows of no personal distinction within the one Being of God), and modalism (the view that the three Persons are successive and not simultaneous modes of God's Being). The inspiring Spirit wonderfully superintended the language of the writers of both Testaments for His own revealing ends.

32 : The Creative Word

Psalm 33

The Old Testament provides a preparation for the fuller revelation of the New in a number of different ways. There are direct predictions, there are typological foreshadowings, and there is the use of theological terms, applied later in a special way to Him in the New Testament. It is with this last that we are to be concerned in this study and the next.

The term 'word' is used of Christ in John 1.1, 14. Any reader of that passage with a Jewish background would at once be led to think of the Old Testament use of the term. In the Old Testament it is used chiefly of the Divine revelation. It is also applied to the creative work of God, however, as in this psalm (6, 9). Gen. 1 also lays much stress upon the function of the Divine word in the creation of the universe.

In this psalm of praise the psalmist seems to be suggesting that it is profitable to relate the revealing and creative words of God in our thinking. In vs. 4 f. he asserts the faithfulness of God's word. What He has said to His people can be relied upon; it can never fail, unlike the ideas which emanate from the hearts of men (10 f.). Of course His word is reliable, for the very foundations of the universe were laid by it (6–9)! We see here how great was the claim of the Saviour when He declared, 'Heaven and earth will pass away, but my words will not pass away' (Matt. **24.**35). The word of God is reliable because it is in a sense an extension of His personality. What a man utters responsibly is really part of himself; 'the thought is the man'. So we are prepared for the great New Testament disclosure that the word of God, creative and revealing, is personal and Divine, and that He, like the creative and revealing word in the Old Testament, is utterly trustworthy.

Meditation: The word of God leads us to trust in the God of the word (18–22).

33 : Divine Wisdom

Proverbs 8

The ancient world valued wisdom as the modern values knowledge. Simply to state the matter thus is to question whether the passing of the centuries has really resulted in the 'coming of age' of the race. In the Old Testament wisdom is always intensely practical; it is of value not for its own sake but for its employment in the daily task of living. In this passage wisdom is personified and she calls upon men to receive instruction (1–21). This wisdom is identical with the fear of the Lord (13, cf. **9.**10; Psa. **111.**10). The Old Testament knows nothing of a wisdom which does not take God into account.

At v. 22 there is an important development in the thought of the chapter. From this point onwards the writer of Proverbs expounds the relationship of wisdom to God. Because the personification is continued from the earlier part of the chapter the impression is created that this is a relationship between two persons. Attention is concentrated upon the creation of the universe, and in it all Wisdom is seen as the 'companion' of God.

The apostle Paul spoke of Christ as the Wisdom of God

(1 Cor. **1**.24, cf. 1 Cor. **1**.30; Col. **2**.3), and it seems that our Lord spoke thus of Himself. 'The utterance of Luke **11**.49 would be clear of ambiguity if by "the wisdom of God" Jesus meant Himself, as indeed Matthew understood Him to do (Matt. **23**.34)' (C. Anderson Scott).

Many Christians in the early centuries assumed from this that Prov. **8** had a straightforward and direct application to Christ. As a result there was considerable argument during the Arian debate in the fourth century concerning the proper translation of Prov. **8**.22. The orthodox argued that it should be rendered 'The Lord possessed me . . .' (cf. AV [KJV]) while the Arians (who denied the deity of Jesus) declared that it should be 'The Lord created me . . .'

The debate as to the correct translation is not over but it is now clear enough that it is of less doctrinal moment than was imagined in the fourth century. The personification of Wisdom in this chapter is a half-way stage between the merely abstract treatment of it and the disclosure that Wisdom has become incarnate in Christ. Prov. **8** does not speak *directly* of Christ but it does prepare for Him. It is worth comparing Psa. **22** (which can be applied in detail to the Saviour) and Psa. **69** (which can be applied only in parts). The latter is quoted in relation to Christ in the New Testament. We can see Christ in it, therefore, in so far as the sufferer depicted is righteous, but we need not feel the necessity of justifying the application of every detail to Him.

> *'Ere God had built the mountains, or raised the fruitful hills;*
>
> *Before He filled the fountains that feed the running rills;*
>
> *In me, from everlasting, the wonderful I AM*
>
> *Found pleasures never wasting, and Wisdom is my name.'*
>
> (*William Cowper*).

Questions and themes for study and discussion on Studies 29–33

1. If the confusion and scattering at Babel was an act of the Triune God, in what ways did it differ from the

strangely similar, and yet in other ways very different, event of Pentecost?

2. In what ways should the appearances of the angel of the Lord be distinguished from the Incarnation?

3. What place should Old Testament anticipations of the Trinity have in the Christian approach to the Jew with the gospel?

4. Consider the relation of the word of God to faith.

5. Compare Prov. 8.32–36 with the teaching of Jesus about the importance of a right attitude towards Himself.

CHARACTER STUDIES

34 : The Shepherd Boy

1 Samuel 16.1–13; Psalm 8

The secret visit of the aged prophet to Bethlehem is told with
brevity, but much may be read between the lines. The old age
of the prophet was a sad and shadowed one. The breach with
Saul was absolute (2), and Saul himself was entering the last
darkened era of his reign, a time of mental illness and fierce
frustration.

The farming community of Bethlehem was full of solidity.
We have walked on its high hills in earlier studies, and met
some of its sturdy peasants and shepherds. We now meet the
household of Jesse, Ruth's grandson. The strong young men
paraded before the prophet, and he looked into the eyes of
each. In no case did he feel that surge of conviction which
he had learned to know as the voice of God.

David was forgotten, and when the messenger sent for
him, out on the very slopes where, a millennium later, 'the
shepherds watched their flocks by night', he came running.
Hence perhaps his 'ruddy' countenance, hot from his race
home. He was handsome, too, a boy with fine eyes (12). So
David, of whose mind and heart more is revealed than of any
other character in the Old Testament, enters the story of the
Bible.

He was good to look upon, but also had a choice mind.
These were the unspoiled days of which perhaps Psa. 8 is one
of the echoes, days of poetry, music, love of the open hills
and the countryside. He was soon to meet Saul, and the tasks
and tests which life had in store for him.

Amid the flood of his self-revelation in the poetry which flowed from him, David never seems to mention the momentous event in the farmhouse at Bethlehem. Perhaps it was unwise to speak of it before jealous brothers (17.28). Jesse himself, such were the perilous times, may have imposed a bond of silence on his family. But in David's conduct, this day and its events most certainly reveal themselves. He lived, all through his greater days, on a mighty faith that he was destined for the throne. Hence his noble abstinence from all violence towards the hostile king. No haste, like Jacob's, was to rend for him the delicate web of God's outworking purposes. So here stood the youth who was to succeed gloriously, fall lamentably, rise again, and in all experience reveal more of God and man than any other figure before Isaiah.

35 : Darkened King

1 Samuel 16.14–23; Galatians 5

Verse 14 reads strangely, and raises again the question earlier discussed (Vol. 2, Study 46)—the 'hardening' of Pharaoh's heart. A Hebrew would not have thought the statement strange, or that it in any way made the Author of All Good the creator simultaneously of evil. God permitted Saul's affliction. To such malady of the mind had the tensions of obstinate self-will led. The end was to be a recognizable paranoia.

It is a solemn fact of human experience that the spirit which will not bend before God sometimes breaks before circumstance. The drive and dash were obviously departing from Saul. In the next chapter he sits helpless and afraid before the challenge of Goliath (17.11). This is not the warrior who led the relief expedition to Jabesh-Gilead. His memory also seems impaired. He knew David as the harp-player of his melancholic hours, but asks Abner who he is (17.55–58). Of course the question might merely be as to David's lineage, a detail naturally enough forgotten. Nor do we know the time lapse between the chapters.

But so it became the ironic lot of the anointed king of Israel to sit and soothe the wild passions of the one who now unworthily sat upon the throne. Thus was David tested. God sometimes imposes strange tasks upon His servants. He calls upon them to serve the thankless and unworthy, to waste time —or so it appears—on fruitless duties, and consume energy and impair health on activities which bring no joy and seem to have little purpose.

The reason is that the fruits of the Spirit (they are listed in the letter to the Galatians) are measured only in the qualities of the soul. These are what God values. David had enormous trials ahead of him, and it was of the first importance that he should learn as a young man to wait, and continue waiting, to trust and to obey. A leader must be practised in obedience, and of all the lessons which man is called upon to learn, that of patience stands to the fore. Touching the strings of the harp in the gloomy presence of the tormented man, David was to learn self-control, pity, endurance . . . Read Browning's poem *Saul*, which magnificently evokes the scene of the king and the harpist.

36 : Goliath

1 Samuel 17

The enormous hoplite of the Philistines was possibly one of the scattered Rephaim (Deut. 2.20–23), a race of extraordinary physique, who had taken refuge with the Philistines, and served as a mercenary in their army. The Philistines were prone to admire a man of strength and stature. Witness their early acceptance of Samson. There is some evidence, from skeletal remains, of the presence of men of exceedingly large stature in Palestine. The length of the cubit is not sure. It depends upon the average size of the human body, an uncertain criterion. According to the measurements of the Siloam Tunnel, the cubit may have been near fifteen inches. Beings of comparable stature have been known. Such stature is sometimes due to an excess of a growth hormone produced by the pituitary gland, a rare but documented phenomenon. The Royal College of Surgeons is said to hold the skeleton of a nine-foot Irishman.

The character of the giant hoplite is clearly depicted, arrogant, blasphemous, mightily enjoying his popularity with his own folk and the fear of the foe. The fruit of such arrogance is over-confidence. Goliath committed the cardinal mistake of underestimating his foe, always a dangerous error.

The result which followed is true to a historical principle of warfare. It is even true to nature. The vast armoured reptiles, who once dominated creation, have all disappeared. The stegosaur, whose forty-foot skeletons may be seen in museum halls, was covered with horn and bone from its tiny head to its mighty tail. It and its like disappeared before new creations, unarmoured, but with greater mobility, greater striking-power, and greater intelligence. So in history. Heavier knights did not sweep the heavy knights away, but longbows at Crécy, and flights of arrows from unmailed bowmen. Not galleons, but swift corvettes, scuttled the Armada. Elephants (read it in the story of the Maccabees) were beaten not by bigger or better elephants, but by brave men with short stabbing spears. So with David. 'Am I a dog,' roared the Philistine, 'that you come to me with sticks?' He threw back his head to laugh. Under the helmet brim, which should have been kept low, the whistling slingstone found the exposed forehead. Greater mobility, and greater striking-power, in the hands of higher intelligence, and a higher morale based on a burning faith, had won the day. David always remembered that moment (Psa. 27.1–3).

37 : Saul's Jealousy

1 Samuel 18.5–22

'Jealousy is cruel as the grave,' says Solomon. 'Its flashes are flashes of fire, a most vehement flame' (Song of Sol. 8.6). We have met jealousy before in Scripture, and seen it for the base and vicious thing it is. Its source is pride and self-esteem, and it seeks to thrust others down that self may be exalted. It sees a threat to security in every success or achievement of another. In Saul's case the vice was fed by the growth of his psychological malady. His deepening paranoia saw rivals everywhere, even in the shepherd boy, who had struck down for him the warrior of Gath, the fearsome Goliath.

Jealousy began in this vivid story with a popular song, not meant to be taken literally, but built on Hebrew parallelism (7). Once entertained, the evil became a habit of thought with Saul, so that David became an object of obsessive hatred. Thought eventually issued in action, as all thought commonly does. All deeds, good or evil, begin in the mind, and Saul's attempt at murder began with thoughts and visions of murder, entertained and cherished in the person. The Lord's teaching in the Sermon on the Mount, that the guilt lies in cherishing and retaining the desire, finds confirmation in the javelin of Saul. He failed to kill David, but bore the load of the desire.

The attempt was unsuccessful, for in David Saul was dealing with a superbly trained athlete. So next came low cunning, another characteristic symptom of Saul's worsening malady. Saul becomes contemptible when he uses his daughter's affection to plot treachery against David, and covers a plot with a show of generosity.

Observe in the whole story David's self-control. Saul was 'raving' in his house (10), but David, obviously without relaxing his caution, bravely sought to calm him with his music. Twice it is remarked (14, 15) that the sorely tried young man behaved with wisdom. He made no attempt, as many a denizen of an Eastern Court might have done, to remove his tormentor by assassination. He ignored the wave of popularity which was running in his favour through the land. He abstained from all retaliation. Such reserve could arise only from a deep, quiet confidence that his times and his person were alike in God's hands. It was one of David's finest hours.

38 : Jonathan the Man

1 Samuel 18.1-5; 19.1-17; 20.1-16

Jonathan has a high place among the characters of the Old Testament. Good, true, valiant, he stands in that tense and corrupt court and household, and under the sad shadow of his father's madness, a figure of integrity and strength. It sometimes falls to a good man's lot to live out his life in dark and evil places, to find his desire for good met with daily frustration, and whose worth seems wasted.

Jonathan's brave championship of David had little abiding influence on Saul, who speedily lapsed into his corroding jealousy, but Jonathan left a noble story in Scripture, which has played its part in the annals of the human spirit. Nor can we guess how much the friendship of the good prince meant to the future king of Israel in his time of testing. Jonathan was well aware that David was to possess his father's kingdom. Nor did he ever question that he owed a debt of loyalty to his father, as well as to his friend. He must have been sombrely aware of the fact that his own life was tangled with his father's doom. Friendship cost him much, and he never used it to his own advantage, never lifted a hand against his father.

But look again at David in this same situation. The thought of Jonathan and his loyalty must have been a cleansing power in the exile's mind. Considering Saul, his madness and his cruelty, David might have been tempted to look with some satisfaction on his own integrity and greater suitability for royal power in Israel. God, he could secretly conclude, had chosen him as a proper substitute for the murderous king. To look at Jonathan was to see such a conclusion crumble. With a man like Jonathan as Saul's natural heir, the choice of David was not nearly apparent. Jonathan, popular with the people of the land, David's equal in military exploits, a nobleman in character as well as in rank, would have made a distinguished king. David was turned to the humbling thought that he was not chosen for any excellence he possessed beyond his friend. He faced the outworking of an inscrutable plan, and could only face it with a plea for help. God had chosen, he knew not why. It was his part to justify the choice.

39 : Jonathan the Friend

1 Samuel 20.17–42

'Never contract friendship,' said Confucius, 'with a man who is not better than yourself.' How this policy could mutually work out is difficult to see, but there is a certain wisdom in the advice. It is possible that, judged by the visible qualities of character, Jonathan was a better man than David.

But note Jonathan's final word: 'The Lord shall be between me and you . . .' (42). The words establish a principle of friendship, relevant in all relationships between one person and another. In all true patterns of human love and fellowship there is a trinity—two persons and their Lord. It is the presence of the Lord which softens all clash of personality and harmonizes differences between man and man, and man and woman. The influence of one person on another, if that influence is mediated through God in a common faith and loyalty, can only produce good. It can never promote evil. God, therefore, becomes the test of all true friendship. If He cannot form a third, any relationship between two people is unblest, unsteady and unhealthy. Jonathan, then, enunciated an eternal truth in his last words to his friend.

The closing words of the vivid story are infinitely sad. Like the Lord 'setting his face steadfastly' to go up to Jerusalem and all that was waiting for Him there, Jonathan turned away, and returned to his duty, and his fate. There was nothing to stop his going into the wilderness with his friend. Between them they could have headed a popular movement. It would have been easy to have rebelled against a father who had used him so ill. But he chose duty, when he chose the road back to the city, and that road led to death. It was a road of sorrow, but it held the peace of God. There is a sense in which Jonathan died for another, and in that choice foreshadowed the very Christ of God.

'We do not choose our own parts in life,' said Epictetus. 'Our simple duty is confined to playing them well.' In such a role the good Jonathan never faltered. And it was Carlyle who said truly: 'Our grand business is not to see what lies dimly in the distance, but to do what lies clearly to hand.' The only clear path for Jonathan at that sad moment was the one down which the lad with the bow and the quiver full of arrows had taken.

40 : David's Desperation

1 Samuel 21.1–9; 22.1–23; Psalm 52

David lied to Ahimelech the priest. He secured help from the innocent man of God by a subterfuge. It was, no doubt, a stratagem of war, and a desperate attempt at self-preservation, but it was none the less an unworthy falsehood, especially in one who knew the will of God, and had learned well some of the lessons of nobler living. In the last words of the story David accepts full responsibility for the grim disaster which fell upon the innocent community, and offers no excuse for himself. He dealt with his fault in the only way in which fault can properly be dealt with. He recognized it for what it was, confessed it, made no attempt to mitigate it, and made every effort to quench the continuing effects.

But it all arose from deception. 'O what a tangled web we weave,' wrote Scott, 'when first we practise to deceive.' It seemed so simple and obvious a piece of trickery, to secure food for his hungry men, and weapons for himself, by a piece of untruthfulness. But he wove a web which enmeshed the lives of a whole innocent little town. Sin is like some virus, entering unseen into a body and ravaging it throughout. 'Sin came into the world through one man' and incidentally by one lie (Gen. 3.4).

David poured some of his feelings into the poetry of a psalm. He had met an evil man, but he was bitterly aware that he had given that evil man an occasion for action. His horror at treachery and the wickedness of the tongue appears in many a psalm, and David must have been aware of how very difficult it is to draw a firm boundary line between the small falsehood which produced the massacre of Nob, and the information which Doeg gave to Saul. Doeg, in fact, spoke the truth, yet used his tongue for evil. Had an untruth not played disastrously into his hand, he would have been impotent to harm.

'Do not let us lie at all,' said Ruskin, 'do not let us think of one falsehood as harmless, another as slight, and another as unintended. Cast them all aside. They are all ugly smoke from the pit, and it is better that our heart should be swept clean of them.'

Questions and themes for study and discussion on Studies 34–40

1. The fruits of the Spirit.

2. How should jealousy in self, or in others against us, be dealt with?

3. The bases of true friendship.

4. Priorities in loyalty.

5. Are there degrees in falsehood?

THE HOLY TRINITY

Old Testament Anticipations of the Trinity (Prophecy)

41 : 'Holy, holy, holy'

Isaiah 6; John 12.37–41

As we saw in Study No. 31 there is often an intimate link between two passages, one in the Old Testament and the other in the New, and the study of the two together enriches our understanding of each. This is certainly true of the present passages.

In the well-known sixth chapter of Isaiah we notice the first personal pronoun (8, cf. note on this in Study No. 29) and the Trisagion, the threefold ascription of holiness to God. These features of the passage would be sufficient in themselves to draw our attention to it. The New Testament exercises its own special constraint upon us in this matter, however, for in John 12.37–41 we have a remarkable commentary upon it.

These verses occupy a place of special importance in the Gospel of John. John has given an account of the public ministry of Jesus in his first twelve chapters. In this ministry a number of signs had been given of His Deity (cf. 20.30 f.), but the Jews as a whole had not responded in faith. John now selects two passages from Isaiah to illustrate their unbelief, one from Isa. 53 (38) and the other from Isa. 6 (40). It is the words of v. 41 which are so significant and startling: 'Isaiah said this when he saw his glory and spoke of him.' These words probably relate to both quotations but if to one

only then they must refer to the second. It is difficult, therefore, to escape from the impression that John means us to
understand Isaiah to have seen the pre-incarnate Christ in his
temple vision. He does not seek to justify this interpretation.
This would seem to imply that his readers would accept it as
valid without any such justification. If this is so, then it
must have been generally accepted in New Testament times
that Christ was pre-existent, that He was God, and that He
could be seen in the manifestations of God in the Old Testament.

*'We laud and magnify Thy glorious name: evermore prais-
ing Thee and saying, holy, holy, holy, Lord God of hosts,
Heaven and earth are full of Thy glory: glory be to Thee,
O Lord most high.'*

(Sursum Corda)

42 : God's Servant and His Spirit

Isaiah 48.9–22

The opening verses of this chapter have much to say about
the sins of the people of Israel. The reader is all prepared for
threats of judgement. Instead the marvel of the Divine
patience and long-suffering is unfolded (8–11). The clause
which ends v. 11 (cf. **42**.8) should be borne in mind when
reading New Testament passages which speak of the glory of
Christ (e.g. Luke **24**.26; 2 Cor. **3**.18–4.6; Heb. **1**.3). Christ is
Himself God. He is the very incarnation of the God who
inspired His prophet to pen these words. For v. 12, see the
note on Isa. **44**.6 in Study No. 18. The references to Babylon
(14,20) show that the deliverance from Exile through Cyrus
(probably referred to in the words, 'the Lord loves him', v. 14)
is chiefly in view here.

There is one verse where there is an abrupt change of
speaker (16). The RSV paragraph system tends to obscure the
abruptness here. Who is the speaker? Is he the prophet?
Many commentators think so. F. D. Kidner declares, however, 'It is more meaningful if it anticipates the "me" of
49.1; **50**.4; **61**.1; in other words, the Servant in whom Jesus
was to see Himself. It is a remarkable glimpse, from afar, of

the Trinity.' The Servant Songs of Isaiah, which consist of at least **42**.1–4; **49**.1–6; **50**.4–9 and **52**.13–**53**.12, start from the nation but focus more and more on an Individual whose mission involved suffering and death for the sins of others and who alone can be in the picture in ch. **53**. It is certainly possible that He speaks in this verse (**48**.16) in preparation for His longer utterance in ch. **49**. On this view the words 'and his Spirit' would constitute a second object rather than a second subject. If this is so (and in fairness it must be said that we cannot be dogmatic), the verse remarkably anticipates Gal. **4**.4, 6, 'But when the time had fully come, God sent forth his Son . . . And because you are sons, God has sent the Spirit of his Son into our hearts . . .'

Verses 17–19 are of great devotional value. Spend some time in meditating on them as you close this study.

43 : The Divine Shepherd

Ezekiel 34

Canaan was largely a pastoral country and it is not surprising that pastoral imagery occurs frequently in the Old Testament. Indeed the figurative use of the word 'shepherd' is much more frequent than its literal use. The term was used of the leaders of Israel, especially by Isaiah, Jeremiah and Zechariah. The present chapter is the most important in Ezekiel on this theme.

The very use of the term sharply differentiates Israel from the nations round about her. Most of the leaders of the great nations which rose and fell in the Middle East had anything but the shepherd outlook, for this implied love and concern for their people. Similarly most of the kings, judges, priests and other leaders of Israel had departed from the Lord so that the very word 'shepherd' constituted an implicit rebuke when used of them (1–10). So, in the passage where He rebukes Israel's shepherds, God declares 'there was no shepherd' (5), for the true shepherd heart was lacking in them all. They would know the judgement of God.

Because all others had failed, God declared that He would take up the work Himself (11–22, 25–31). The wording of

v. 11 lays exceptional emphasis upon the person of the
Divine Shepherd: 'I, I myself' (cf. v. 20). This reminds us
of the emphatic 'I' in John 10.11, which we might render 'I,
even I, am the good shepherd.' Indeed, so many of the
utterances of Jesus which reveal His shepherd heart remind
us of this passage (e.g. cf. Mark 6.34; Luke 12.32; John
10.1–18, 26 f.). The story of Zacchaeus in Luke 19 ends with
words which, without the term itself, certainly contain the
shepherd idea: 'For the Son of Man came to seek and to save
the lost.' In Jesus the great God Himself became flesh in
order to seek and to save the lost, and this constituted a
rebuke to the 'shepherds' of the day, the Pharisees and
Sadduccees.

Ezekiel also refers to the setting up of the Messianic
Shepherd over them (23 f.). This does not appear at first sight
to be consistent with God's emphatic assertions that He
would act as Shepherd *personally*, but the New Testament
doctrine of the Messiah's Deity (anticipated in passages like
Isa. 7.14; 9.6) provides us with the key. God is Shepherd;
the Messiah is Shepherd; both statements are true, for the
Messiah is God manifest in the flesh.

'Perverse and foolish oft I strayed; but yet in love He
   sought me,
And on His shoulder gently laid, and home rejoicing
   brought me.'

(Henry Williams Baker)

44 : With them . . . by His Spirit

Haggai 2.1–9

The return from Babylonian Exile was very much like a new
Exodus. Haggai prophesied soon after the return, and like
Zechariah, he sought to encourage the people to press on with
the work of rebuilding the Temple in Jerusalem. The secular
and religious leaders were Zerubbabel and Joshua respectively
(1.1, 12, 14; 2.2, 4).

The name Joshua was an honoured one in the history of
the people of Israel. It had been borne by the great leader
who had first introduced their fathers to this land to which

they had so recently returned. Three times over the Lord had said to him, 'Be strong and of good courage' (Josh. 1.6 f., 9), and had assured him that He would be with him just as He had been with Moses before him (Josh. 1.5, 9). This new Joshua and his compatriots needed the same assurance, and God exhorts them in a threefold way to 'take courage' (4). Many hundreds of years had gone by since the Exodus and the first entry into the land. Nevertheless God assured them through Haggai that the promise of His presence, so real to Moses and to Joshua, was as firm as ever. It had not been set aside through the passing of the years (4 f., cf. Exod. 29.45).

What is of special interest to us in this study is the reference to the Spirit of God (5). There is no promise of the presence of the Spirit with the people of Israel as a whole in the Pentateuch. Therefore, this passage is really an interpretation of the promise that God's presence would go with them. He would be with them through His Spirit. So the statements, 'I am with you' (4) and 'My Spirit abides among you' (5) are virtually identical (cf. Psa. 139.7). In most Old Testament references to the Spirit of God He is seen to be the Agent of God, but here He is more. This then is a preparation for the New Testament doctrine of the Spirit and His relationship to the Father.

The promise about the greater glory of the new temple (7–9) may perhaps also remind us that even this temple was destined ultimately to pass away (Matt. 23.38–24.2). It was to be replaced by the temple of His body, laid down in death (John 2. 19–22) and raised up, so that in Him the Church would rise, His mystical body, 'a holy temple in the Lord' (Eph. 2.18–22). The Spirit of God would indwell this temple, for now temple and people of God would be one.

45 : The Coming Judge

Malachi 3

The discouragement which many of the returned exiles experienced in Haggai's day deepened into disillusionment by the time of Malachi almost 100 years later (in Nehemiah's day), and a general mood of scepticism seemed to descend upon the people. This finds expression in utterances like 'How hast thou loved us?' (1.2); 'What a weariness this is' (1.13); 'Everyone who does evil is good in the sight of the Lord, and he delights in them'; 'Where is the God of justice?' (2.17); and 'It is vain to serve God' (3.14).

The questions of 2.17 are answered by God in ch. 3, and especially in vs. 1–6. The coming day of judgement will reveal that He is indeed a God of justice and that He cares about righteousness. This day will be heralded by God's own messenger (1a). These words are applied in the New Testament to John the Baptist (Matt. 11.10 f., etc.), who prepared the way of Christ and warned men to flee from the coming judgement of God.

Reference to the quotation in Matthew will reveal that when our Lord applied these words to John the Baptist He altered them somewhat. 'Before me' becomes 'Before my face'. This is a phenomenon known as *Midrash Pesher*, which was employed by the rabbis and was used extensively by the community of the Dead Sea Scrolls. It was a combination of quotation with interpretation. It only seems peculiar to us because it does not accord with our own conventions of quotation. Our Lord's implied interpretation shows clearly a belief in His own deity, which was shared also by Mark (Mark 1.1–3).

It would seem that 'the Lord whom you seek' and 'the messenger of the covenant' are identical, the second phrase being best understood as in apposition to the first. This 'messenger of the covenant' will be the 'angel of the Lord', for the English words 'messenger' and 'angel' translate the same Hebrew word. Christ came in this way to judge (an earnest of the great judgement) in His cleansing of the Temple. God will give His people another opportunity to return to Him (6–12) and so to experience His blessing. The Lord was not unaware of the fact that there were some who had been faithful to Him despite the cynicism with which they were surrounded (13–18).

Questions and themes for study and discussion on Studies 41–45

1. If the pre-incarnate Christ can be recognized in Isa. 6 can He be recognized in every Old Testament manifestation of God?

2. 'The word "sent" as applied to the Son and the Spirit suggests a great mystery—the humility of God.' Meditate on this.

3. What does God do for His people Himself, and not through a mere created agent?

4. What difference should the presence of the Spirit of God with me make to my approach to my daily work?

5. In what ways are we likely, although not literally of his kin, to be 'sons of Jacob' (Mal. 3.6)?

CHARACTER STUDIES

46 : David in Exile

1 Samuel 21.10–15; 27.1–12; 29.1–11

It is difficult to sort out the chronology of David's time among the Philistines. On the face of it the book seems to record two periods among them, and the matter is of no great historical importance. We are seeking the personalities of Scripture, and here, without doubt, is an unexpected facet of character revealed.

The months spent at Gath were among the darkest of David's life. He was leagued with his people's enemies. He could be described in very truth as a traitor to his own. But note that we are clearly told that this was David's day of hopelessness and despair (27.1). Like other characters in the Bible, he was walking after the devices of his own heart. Not David the godly, but David the backslider walks before us, for the Bible is ruthless in revealing the faults of those who have added the brightest chapters in its story. It never hides the truth. And who are we to cast a stone? Let us remember further that the outlaw of these unhappy days was the ruddy youth who once, in joy and innocence, kept his father's sheep. Hate and jealousy in the hearts of those who should have loved and honoured him had done this damage to him. Furthermore, he paid, as men always must pay, in the inevitable justice of things, for these backslidings. His hand was declared unfit to build the house of the Lord he so passionately desired to see. And let us also remember, in this and all such cases, that the One who knows the agony in the sinner's mind alone can truly judge his sin. David came back. He won the final victory.

70

This truth must be borne in mind in interpreting the many utterances of praise for David in Scripture. For example, 1 Kings 11.4 f. (AV[KJV]) speaks of David walking before God with a 'perfect' heart. How can this be justified in one so obviously faulty? 'Perfection' of heart does not, however, suggest sinlessness, but whole-heartedness and singleness of purpose. David is visibly imperfect, and the Bible is as ruthless with his imperfections as it is with those of Jacob and Peter. His story stands in Scripture as a warning, as well as an inspiration. David paid, and paid again, for his sin. David was a man after God's heart, because he knew repentance, because he could bow with humility beneath chastening, and because his life was fed on a faith in a grand unfolding Plan.

47 : David in Adullam

Psalm 34

Man, as old Samuel was warned in Jesse's farmhouse, looks on the outward appearance of a man (1 Sam. 16.7), God sees 'the hidden part'. It is easy to be harsh with David for his retreat to Gath, but fortunately, in his case, we have more than the story of events. David was a poet, and a man of prayer. He poured into his poetry both the jubilation and the agony of his heart.

Driven out with scorn by the enemies of his people, he found the clean wilderness again. In the cave with two openings and a spring of water, where he made his guerrilla headquarters in the rough Judean hills, the exile realized how good God has been to him. In this revealing psalm we can guess what happened in his distraught and tormented mind during the days of his humiliation. In it we see how his faith held beneath his dark backsliding, and what convictions stayed him from complete self-destruction.

Abimelech was, of course, Achish. Like Pharaoh and Caesar, the word had become a dynastic title. Achish had dismissed David with contempt. The shame turned to thankful joy. It was an answer to prayer (4), dim and fumbling though prayer must have been in those days of sad disgrace. David knew where to look (5), in other words, in whom to put his ultimate trust. And catch the note of pure confession in the next verse (6). David had failed because he had not 'looked' in the right direction. Circumstances, besetting trouble, the harsh treacheries of men, had held his eyes. There is one only to fear (9), and fear in such a context is no degrading terror, but a reverence compounded of love, loyalty, and faith. This is the emerging lesson from the dark experience of Gath (11). Men should fear not the malice or the machinations of men, but rather the peril of leaving the circle of God's protection. Back in the great cave, David could almost imagine God's messenger standing sentinel (7) at the cave's mouth. He had learned a lesson he was to learn again, in circumstances yet more bitter, that God can do nothing with pride and self-sufficiency (18; Psa. 51.17).

This is an alphabetical psalm. To aid in memorizing, each verse is made to begin with a letter of the Hebrew alphabet. David has two letters left, so he sets forth the two truths which had thrust themselves on his perceptive mind in the days of his humiliation—the suicidalness of evil (21), and the completeness of God's salvation (22; Rom. 8.1).

48 : David and the Ziphites

1 Samuel 23; Psalm 54

The chronicler describes a month of warfare, David's blow for the country he loved, though its king had rejected him, the brief reappearance of Jonathan in the story, Jonathan who had caught a breath of hope, and the treachery of the men of Ziph. Treachery, as many a psalm bears witness, stirred David to the depths. He was a man of deep loyalties, and found the vicious betrayal of men a difficult fault to understand or to forgive. He was to know much of it.

It was a close call for David. The guerrilla fighter avoids active confrontation, but Saul had David at bay, when the Philistine enemy came into the hill country on one of his perennial raids, and the king was compelled to pull back the experienced army units which his hatred had committed to the combing of the wilderness for the fugitive. David took the opportunity thus offered to withdraw deeper into the wild country towards the Dead Sea.

In the wilderness David knew his best days. Down among the wadis, crags and cliffs of the Judean ranges, David learned some of the deeper lessons of faith, patience and calm confidence in God which infuse his psalms. Adversity can be creative when prosperity benumbs. Adversity is often the straightest path to truth. 'Adversity is like the period of the former and the latter rain,' said Sir Walter Scott, 'cold, comfortless, unfriendly. Yet from that season have their birth the flower and the fruit, the date and the rose.' Sir Philip Sidney echoes from an earlier century: 'The truly great and good, in affliction bear a countenance more princely than they are wont. It is the temper of the highest hearts, like the palm tree, to strive most upward when most burdened.'

It is also a truth, evident from the psalms of David's creative years, that anything committed in complete faith to God can be transmuted into good. The psalm set down above sprang from the sombre experience of betrayal. Observe the complete surrender of the evil thing to God's transforming hands (1), the resort to prayer (2), the fact of experience (3) set over against a calm faith (4), and the emerging confidence which speaks of the objects of petition as already granted (6 f.). This is faith in its strength and its tranquillity. It was born of a day of trouble.

49 : David and Saul

1 Samuel 24

The cave could have been Adullam, for the geography of the chapter is vague. Saul was on his way to scour Engedi, but the cave where he met David was on the way there (3), and the encounter was unexpected. If the Adullam cave is correctly identified, it had two entrances, and this would account for the boldness of the guerrilla band in the presence of the enemy commando-force. They knew that they could rapidly melt away into the wild hills behind.

Observe David's sensitive mercy. Saul was the Lord's anointed. David knew that he was rejected and that he himself had been chosen to succeed to the royal throne. And yet such was his faith at this time of testing that he refused

to lift a finger to promote his own manifest destiny. He had
learned the lesson that time-bound man finds it most difficult
to learn, that God acts in His own good time, that it is best
to wait for that time, and that patience and endurance are
qualities rich in good and blessing.

David's words (9–15) are full of grace and courtesy. They
touched a responsive chord in the distraught enemy's heart.
Sanity and peace return briefly to Saul, and he speaks with
love and contrition. For a brief time he is near to God
and to restoration. The scales fall from his eyes and he
sees himself for what he is, and recognizes the worth of
the man he was hunting in bitterness of soul. His speech is
full of pathos.

David knew that such repentance was not likely to endure.
He had seen the undulations of mood in the tormented man.
He was aware that those whom he could trust were the rough
and determined men who had gathered to him in the wilderness (22.2), and that the king would keep no covenant or pact.
For the meantime the hunt was over. Saul, in brief penitence,
withdrew his task-force, and David disappeared into the hills
to await his day.

It is a sad chapter, but it shows David in one of his finest
hours, sensitive to the movements of God's will, tranquil in
his assurance, strong, forbearing, kind. Perhaps Shakespeare
had the passage in mind when he said that mercy 'becomes
the throned monarch better than his crown.' In David's mind
the crown could wait.

50 : David's Faith (1)

Psalm 27

This period of David's life is rich in psalms. Some of them
bear ancient rabbinical headings which link the utterance or
prayer with some specific experience. Psa. 57 is thus identified,
and the tradition behind the identification must be accorded
the respect which tradition not uncommonly merits. In the
case of other psalms we can only hazard a conjecture, but
there are quite a handful which bear the marks of David's
wilderness meditations. Of these we might pick out two or

74

three for comment, as we seek to know the man who became the second and the greatest king of Israel, and also one of the great religious poets of all time.

Look at Psa. **27**. Some great deliverance has taken place, and it has grown out of past triumph. Catch the echoes of Goliath (2; 1 Sam. **17**.41–58). Similarly, David told Saul on that occasion about his prowess with the bear. Victory, as is commonly the case, was born of victory. In the moral sphere the first fight is the most important. If defeat comes there, it is likely to be permanent.

Mark the imagery of the opening words. First comes light. Faith knows what it is about (John **11**.8–10). Its principles are sharp and clear (Gen. **39**.9). Its goal is plain to see (Phil. **3**.14). Second comes salvation, strong in the thought of one who had just escaped some net of evil, salvation from evil circumstance (5), despair (6), calumny (12). Third comes strength. Weakness spawns cowardice, frustration, defeat.

And all this flows from the grand thought that God cares, plans, loves. High on some crag (5), watching his baffled foes far below him in the ravine, David sees in one moment of dazzling truth the most important fact in life—there is a God who is love. The AV(KJV) is closer to the Hebrew than the RSV in v. 13, provided the unnecessary main clause in italics ('I had fainted') is omitted. Looking down on the trap he has evaded, David gasps without rounded syntax, and in an unfinished sentence: '. . . unless I had believed to see the goodness of the Lord in the land of the living.' The main clause can be filled in by each who can echo that prayer, according to his own circumstances.

Therefore, he concludes, wait for God, and he was soon to make that theme the subject of a whole psalm, which we shall look at in the next study.

51 : David's Faith (2)

Psalm 37

'Wait for the Lord,' David concluded in the closing verse of yesterday's reading, 'be strong and let your heart take courage; yea, wait for the Lord!' The wild jubilation of that psalm has passed. The psalm which forms today's reading conforms more closely to Wordsworth's definition of poetry: 'Poetry is the spontaneous overflow of powerful feelings. It takes its origin from emotion recollected in tranquillity.'

In this psalm David reaches the same firm conclusion (34) by a quieter path. Why must a man 'wait for the Lord'? Because God's blessings are the reward of faith. They tarry. God's blessings, too, are part of a wider pattern, which requires time to weave itself. Abraham's story is a rich illustration. Again, God's blessings come only when we are ready to understand them. Moses was an illustration.

David is writing here of absolute trust (2 Tim. 1.12), complete committal of mind, heart, life to God, believing that He can control, overrule, transmute circumstances and experience, and so enrich the life. It is not merely a passive state. It is active: 'Trust in the Lord, and do good' (3).

Thus the believer 'delights' in Him (4), and takes pleasure in doing His will. Service can be dour (Mal. 3.13–15) and sour (Luke 15.29). Unwilling service carries no promise. Willing service is rewarded with 'the desires of the heart'. And what are they? The 'heart' in the imagery of the Bible is the core of the personality. And what do we there, in the redeemed centre of our being, desire? Purity, peace, power, confidence, courage? What do we want when nearest to Christ, and in our most solemn moments? Surely nothing less than the will of God in our lives.

'Commit your way . . .' (5). Let us paraphrase vs. 5 f.: 'Trust God to take over career, home, work, circumstances, ambitions and all else, and He will so mould events that your deepest and purest desires shall find fulfilment beyond your dreams, and that life will be filled with the most glorious satisfaction.'

'Be still before the Lord . . .' (7). Thus resting involves the mind, the imagination, the will (Isa 26.3). It means sometimes taking our hands off events as David did in the cave. It means ceasing to strive and leaving vindication (6) and deliverance to God. And remember that this psalm was written by a harried, hunted fugitive.

52 : David's Faith (3)

Psalm 57

This psalm is dated. The heading might more exactly read: 'when he fled from Saul into the cave.' The cave was his guerrilla headquarters at Adullam. The wild place had its lessons. Some storm in the mountains (1), and a remembered word of Moses (Deut. 32.11; cf. Matt. 23.37), provide a train of thought. The storm in David's life was the threat of death (3), the violence of men (4), slander, to which he was always peculiarly sensitive (4), and treachery (6), which always horrified and depressed him.

The remedy was to rest in God. 'In thy strong hands I lay me down . . .' There is no parallel in all ancient literature, outside the Old Testament, for this thought of God as a refuge and a tender protector. Doggedly, steadfastly (7, 10), David holds to the thought that a purpose (2) is working out through all that takes place (Rom. 8.28), a purpose no malice could defeat.

Steadfastness is the keyword of the psalm. 'Stead' is an old word in English for 'place'. 'In my stead'; 'instead of . . .'; 'bedstead'; 'homestead', all illustrate it. 'Steadfast' means, therefore, 'firm in its proper place'. Steadfastness of heart means unshakeable resolution, and immovable faith in the centre of the personality, a stance unassailable (Eph. 6.13 f.).

Note how the psalm breaks through to jubilation. It was probably written close in time to the psalm which precedes it, for, as it may be often observed in the psalms, there are word-echoes and repetitions of theme. Look through the two psalms together and list these phenomena. Psa. 56 ends, to be sure, with a word of quiet victory, a moving prayer which is better read in the AV than in the RSV. This psalm bursts out like a mountain spring into a shout of triumph. The singer goes outside the cave, looks to the high sailing clouds, and sees God's love high as the dome of the sky, and 'steadfast' as his own faith. This is the fourth time in this psalm (RSV) that the adjective has occurred. 'Steady then—keep cool and pray' (1 Pet. 4.7—Moffatt).

Questions and themes for study and discussion on Studies 46–52

1. 'A man after God's own heart.'

2. Deception in Philistia. Is it still practised?

3. 'Sweet are the uses of adversity'.

4. God's plan in our lives. Suppose we frustrate it? Has He alternatives?

5. 'God is Light'. What of guidance?

6. '. . . unless I had believed . . .' (Psa. 27.13, AV [KJV]). Fill in several main clauses.

7. 'Lord, make haste to save us'. Consider this prayer in the light of Psa. 37.

THE HOLY TRINITY

Plurality in Unity (New Testament History)

53: The Eternal Word

John 1.1–5, 14–18

The Greek word 'logos' translated as 'Word' in the main English versions was widely used at the time the Gospel of John was written. The Stoic philosophers were fond of it and thought of it as the Divine principle giving coherence and meaning to everything in the universe. Hermeticism was a doctrine of salvation by revelation from the gods which was taught in Alexandria, and its teachers also used the term. Philo, a philosophical Jew of Alexandria and an older contemporary of our Lord, uses it over thirteen hundred times in his writings without consistent meaning. He tends to personify it and treat it as 'a middle term between God and the world'.

It is not to such sources as these that we should go for our primary understanding of it, however. John was a Jewish Christian and so it is to the Old Testament that we need to go to understand his background. There the word of God is seen to be creative (Gen. 1.3; Psa. 33.6, 9, cf. Study No. 32), revealing (as in its extremely frequent use in the prophets) and eternal (Psa. 119.89). All these ideas appear in the great Prologue (1.1–18) to the Gospel of John. A reader of philosophical bent reading the Gospel would undoubtedly have been stimulated by the use of the term 'logos' in its prologue, and so would find himself coming to the feet of Him who is the incarnation of truth.

As the Word of God, the Son (this more personal term is also used in the Prologue: 14, 18) is eternal. He was 'in the beginning' (1), an expression surely intended to remind the Jewish reader of Gen. **1**.1. He was in the beginning, in fact, as the Agent of creation (3). He was 'with God' (1). The preposition used in this phrase is a common one, although not in the sense it bears here. It could include the idea of fellowship: 'the Word was facing towards God' (cf. 'in the bosom of the Father', 18).

The most striking expression of all, however, is the simple statement 'The Word was God'. Attempts to reduce the significance of this to 'the Word was a god' betray a faulty understanding of Greek. The omission of the definite article in this kind of sentence was normal even though the noun was really definite. It also shows a failure to appreciate that for a Jew 'a god' could only mean a pagan deity, and so no god at all. So the Gospel's introduction prepares us for its climax in the confession of Thomas (**20**.28). Here then is One distinct from God and yet utterly one with Him, and, as God, the source of life and light (4, 5) and grace and truth (16–18) for men.

'Thou art the everlasting Word, the Father's only Son;
God manifestly seen and heard, and heaven's beloved One.
Worthy, O Lamb of God, art Thou that every knee to Thee
*   should bow.'*

(Josiah Conder)

54 : The Great 'I AM'

John 8.48–59

This section of the Gospel of John comes at the close of a controversy between Jesus and the Jews (**8**.31–58), the main theme of which is sonship and its implications. The Jews claim to be children of Abraham (39). Jesus has already agreed that they are his children (37) in the purely physical sense but denies that they are in the sense of bearing his likeness (39 f.). They then claim to be children not only of Abraham but of God (41). Jesus declares that their character belies this and says their spiritual kinship is with Satan (42–44). The claim of

Jesus that those who keep His word will never see death (51) suggests to them a claim to be greater than Abraham and the prophets, whose lives had been terminated by death (53).

At the close of the whole discussion, Jesus declares, 'Truly, truly, I say to you, before Abraham was, I am' (58). No assertion could be greater than this, and they seek to stone Him. What exactly does He mean? He employs the expression translated 'I am' very frequently in this Gospel. He uses it in many of His great assertions: 'I am the bread of life' (6.35); 'I am the door' (10.9); 'I am the good shepherd' (10.14); etc. He sometimes employs it absolutely, as in 8.24, 28; 13.19; for in none of these does the word 'he' occur in the original. He also employs it in 18.5, 8, where it seems at first that He is simply declaring Himself to be Jesus of Nazareth. This cannot account for the reaction of His hearers, however (18.6). It would seem that this simple statement of His identity was uttered in such a manner that it suggested a much deeper claim to His hearers. In fact, the words as used by Him remind us of Exod. 3.14, where God reveals Himself to Moses as the 'I AM'. This is more even than a claim to pre-existence (which could be true of some supernatural, angelic figure). If He had intended this He could have said simply, 'Before Abraham was, I was.' But the use of the present tense suggests that He is the timeless God. The Jews threw stones; the Christian worships.

55 : The Father and the Son

John 10.22–39

One of the most striking features of our Lord's teaching is the way He speaks of Himself as the Son of God. The terms 'Father' and 'Son' appear with very great frequency in the Gospel of John but they are present in His teaching in the other Gospels also (cf. especially Matt. 11.25–27; Luke 10.21 f.). It is true that He taught His disciples to regard God as their Father but He never links His Sonship and theirs by speaking of 'our Father'. The Lord's Prayer was given to the disciples; there is no evidence He ever prayed it Himself. Indeed it was hardly appropriate, for it assumed the presence of sin in the one making its words his own (Matt. 6.12). After His resur-

rection He spoke of 'My Father and your Father'. If His
Sonship had been like theirs it would be difficult to explain
such phraseology.

In our present passage the theme of the power of Christ
is very much to the fore. He speaks of His works, done in
His Father's name (25, cf. 32, 37 f.) and of His ability to
keep His sheep secure and safe (27 f.). His audience would
have no difficulty with His assertion that the Father was all-
powerful and could guarantee their safety (29), but they
would query His own claim to such power. Jesus forestalls
questions on the subject by declaring 'I and the Father are
one'.

What do these words mean? Some have maintained that
they simply indicate oneness of will or purpose. If this were
so, we could not account either for the action of the Jews (31)
or the discourse which follows. In the context they mean
oneness of power, and, as the Jews readily saw, to be one
in power with the Almighty One is to be in essence God.
This does not mean that He and the Father are identical
Persons (for the Father can be spoken of as dwelling in the
Son, and the Son is seen as doing His Father's works, 38).

The passage taken as a whole, then, teaches distinction of
person but unity of essence. This is a great mystery because
there is not true human analogy to this, for all forms of
fellowship fall short of this essential oneness. It would be
a great surprise, however, if we could fully comprehend the
being of God! Could a Being without mystery really be God?

*Meditation : The Christ who gives me eternal life is the
Son of God, and I am safe in Him.*

56 : Lying to the Holy Spirit

Acts 5.1–11

The New Testament is full of teaching about the Person
of Christ and about His relationship to God the Father. There
is an embarrassment of riches here. The same is not true of
the Person of the Holy Spirit. One reason for this is that the
New Testament references to the Spirit quite understandably
concentrate upon His work. Nevertheless the evidence we

have points unerringly towards One who was truly personal and truly Divine.

However we understand the blasphemy against the Spirit it is clear from the passage in which this is referred to (Matt. 12.28–32) that the Spirit is a Divine Person. The very word 'blasphemy' is hardly applicable properly to any other. The assertion that blasphemy against Him is not open to forgiveness in the way that blasphemy against the Son of Man is, establishes His deity beyond question, once we have accepted the deity of Jesus.

In our present passage the sin of Ananias and Sapphira is described as a 'lie to the Holy Spirit' (3) and putting Him 'to the test' (9, NEB). Such language certainly shows that He is a personal being, Indeed, a study of the language used of Him in the Acts provides quite an unshakeable biblical argument for His personality, for the verbs are nearly all ones that can only be used of persons. Follow this up for yourself. But He is not only a Person; He is God. To lie to the Spirit and to lie to God are alternative ways of saying the same thing (3 f.). This was why the punishment meted out to Ananias and his wife was so severe. We cannot deceive the all-seeing One.

Questions and themes for study and discussion on Studies 53–56

1. It has been said that it is important to balance biblical metaphors with each other. Ponder this in relation to the following quotation: 'The title Son may obviously imply later origin and a distinction amounting to ditheism. It is balanced by the other title Logos, which implies eternity and inseparable union. Neither title exhausts the relations. Neither may be pressed so far as to exclude the other' (J. F. Bethune-Baker).

2. Consider the 'I am's' of Jesus in the Fourth Gospel in the light of His deity and the fullness of divine provision for you which they imply.

3. 'If you are the Christ, tell us plainly' (John 10.24). 'He had again and again told the same truth, though the actual word had never crossed His lips while speaking to them' (H. W. Watkins). How then had He told them?

4. Can a true Christian lie to the Holy Ghost?

CHARACTER STUDIES

57 : Nabal

1 Samuel 25

Nabal was a descendant of old Caleb, but he was a drunken churl (3, 36). The success of any guerrilla movement depends upon the support of the countryside and the goodwill of the population at large. This axiom may be illustrated from all history. David and his men had sought to earn the goodwill of the shepherds of the Shephelah. After all, they were a police force (15 f.) against the perennial raiding from both the desert hinterlands and the coastal plain. David did not run Nabal into danger near the area where Saul was active. He sought some sustenance from his plenty away to the north in Carmel, where Nabal had property. But the man was a boor (17), unworthy of his wife, a clever woman who had the confidence of her husband's men.

Nabal died of heart failure (36–38), but he died as he had lived. Lack of courtesy is lack of love, and lack of love is lack of God. Courtesy is a Christian virtue. It is a gift of our faith to our way of life, and boorish Nabal is a warning and a lesson. 'The small courtesies of life', once hailed by Laurence Sterne, are said to be on the wane.

The crowd, inseparable from urban living, can press hard against the defences of life—on the congested road, in the packed supermarket, in the inevitable queue and in the hundred places where man impedes, and so frustrates, his fellows. Delay, obstruction, inefficiency and a seeming unconcern for others, try the patience, fray the temper and put sharpness into the voice and impatience into action. Courtesy becomes a casualty, because courtesy requires serenity, and calls for self-command.

A decay of courtesy could have a cause more sinister than a deteriorating human environment. Perhaps the spirit of man betrays a certain weariness. Old standards of conduct, for more than one unhappy reason, have been abandoned. The Christian faith is under mindless assault.

There is a species of rebellion which finds a perverted satisfaction in damaging old traditions. Sometimes, for all the bandying of the word love in such social contexts, regard for the feelings, the ease and the ideals of others—and they are all elements of love—is the missing factor. It was Belloc who said:

> Of Courtesy—it is much less
> Than courage of heart or holiness;
> Yet in my walks it seems to me
> That the Grace of God is in courtesy.

Belloc had in mind Francis of Assisi, who said: 'Courtesy is one of the properties of God, who gives His rain to the just and unjust by courtesy. Courtesy is the sister of charity by which hatred is vanquished and love is cherished.' Churlish Nabal and gracious Abigail are worth a steady look.

58 : David and Saul Again

1 Samuel 26

Slander had been at work again. David hated it. Saul entertained it. David knew this. Hence his earlier distrust of Saul, now sadly justified. David's curse on slanderers (19) echoes through all time. He who by lies stirs another to evil action bears the burden of the guilt. David's magnificent forbearance is equally for our instruction. 'Devotion', wrote William Law relevantly, 'signifies a life given to God. He is a devout man who lives no longer to his own will, but to the sole will of God, who makes all the parts of his common life parts of piety by doing everything in the name of God.'

Abishai's advice (8) was no doubt a strong temptation. Saul had been spared, and had sinned again with arrogant disregard of mercy shown and the covenant implied. But David was living, in these stirring and momentous days, close to God. He wanted nothing less than the will of God in his life. At such moments he touches the grace of Christ. The lessons of Psa. 37 were being gloriously applied to difficult circumstances.

It is a splendidly told story, this account of the breathless raid on the sleeping camp. It was an act of astonishing courage, and should have stirred Saul to genuine and final repentance. But David still 'went his way' (25), withholding his trust. To trust God is not to abandon the salutary exercise of reason. God guides through the qualities with which He has endowed the mind. The land must have been seething with treachery. The old tribal jealousies and animosities were still just below the surface. They had bedevilled the days of the judges. In the next century they were to divide the land. The evil men of Ziph were not the only group willing to surrender David to Saul.

The Christian does well not to trust the world. He does well who insulates himself from the control of secular society. There are entanglements which turn to snares. The Christian cannot expect ultimate justice from a world which denied it to Christ. Like his Lord, he should not 'commit himself to them' (John 2.24).

59 : Saul's Twilight

1 Samuel 28.3–25

This attack was no common raid. The Philistines had often penetrated the hill-country, looting hamlets and driving off flocks. This time, they sought a wider conquest. The coastal strip was becoming too narrow for them, and they were obviously looking with covetous eyes on the rich plain of Esdraelon or Jezreel, scene of the old victories of Barak and Gideon. Watching the twinkling camp fires of the Philistines from the surrounding ramparts of the hills, Saul saw the coming of the end (4 f.).

The irony of the situation was that history gave clear direction. Had Saul risen to the vast occasion, Gideon's victory

86

and Barak's too might have told him that, if God stood with him, the number of his men or their armaments was of small consequence. But was God with him? This was a question for which Saul, with his defective view of God, had no clear answer. God is not a power to be tapped at the whim of any man, and for long years Saul had scorned God's will in his life, and refused to acknowledge His control. That man's fate is a grim one to whom God says in the end: 'Thy will be done.' Saul was desperate.

Endor lay on the lip of the hills overlooking the plain, and a woman in the village practised the sinister arts of necromancy. It is impossible to explain Saul's vision of Samuel in the language of human experience. The woman, like all her kind, was a charlatan, but it does not seem possible to explain all the phenomena associated with such tamperings with psychic matters by the resources of trickery and deceit. Whatever lay behind the eerie experience, God used it to say His last word to Saul. He listened aghast.

He hears that the morrow is the end. He hears, too, that the nation and his sons shall fall. It is impossible to isolate evil. An act of wrong can be confined neither to time nor place. The lives of men are interwoven, and sin in any personality infects a wider area than that of the life which is its host.

The sight of her broken king stirred some human pity in the weird woman who had been used in this final tragedy. She hurried and prepared Saul's last meal. In the darkened hut on the hillside, the man who might have been a great man ate of the pathetic creature's meat and bread, and, like Judas, went out into the night.

60 : David's Raid

1 Samuel 30

Free from his disastrous entanglement with the Philistines which we have earlier discussed, David regained his old strength and vigour of mind. It is a little difficult to sort out the chronology of these chapters. The last verse of the earlier chapter seems to set David's emancipation from his compromising service just before the northern drive to Jezreel, in repelling which Saul was to lose his life.

The guerrilla band found immediate work at hand. It was a vast opportunity for the Amalekites of the southern desert. Saul had denuded the southern frontiers, and marched his available troops north to face the deep Philistine penetration. The Philistines, too, had stripped their borderlines. The Amalekite savages fell on Ziklag, and took away the families of David's fighting men. They were the nomads of the wilderness whom, long years before, Saul had been called upon to eliminate. The fate of the sick Egyptian (13) is a pointer to their inhumanity and baseness.

Perhaps it was an answer to desperate prayer from the captives that God intervened and plucked David and his band from their Philistine compromise. The callous raiders, directed by the victim of their cruelty, soon had the finest band of fighting-men in Israel on their tracks. In their camp was merrymaking. The wild Bedouin had raided successfully into both the territory of the coastal Philistines, and into the hill country of the Hebrews. David's commandoes fell on them and scattered them.

The real David, royal, generous, confident, seems to emerge in the division of the spoil from the successful raid. He established a principle of reward (24) which has its place in Christian service. It is the will to serve rather than the visible achievement of service which matters, and, as C. S. Lewis once remarked, it is part of the courtesy of Heaven to regard the desire as equal to the deed. Consciousness of a great deliverance, a sudden glow of recovered freedom, and fellowship with God renewed, brought David the mood of generosity and jubilation which seems to flash through the ending of this story. Ziklag was in ashes and it was well destroyed. It was the symbol of failure, retreat and compromise.

61 : Saul's Ending

1 Samuel 31

Archaeology has confirmed the deep northern penetration of the Philistines around this period. Altars bearing characteristic

Cretan features date from 1100 to 1050 B.C, and seem to mark at least a generation of Philistine occupation.

And on Mount Gilboa Saul fought his last fight, and fell with his sons under the Philistine arrows. Saul was a tragic figure. He had qualities of strength and heroism, and in his hour of shame and disaster the men of Jabesh-Gilead remembered what he had done for them, bravely raided Bethshan, and brought the bodies of the king and his sons home for burial.

It is the end which matters. It is the end which all should keep in view. Masefield makes this a haunting thought in Saul Kane's colourful mind. He pictured the 'white unwritten book'—

> *A book that God will take, my friend,*
> *As each goes out at journey's end . . .*
>
> .   .   .   .
>
> *The book he lent is given back*
> *All blotted red and smutted black . . .*
>
> .   .   .   .
>
> *I wondered then why life should be,*
> *And what would be the end of me*
> *When youth and health and strength were gone,*
> *And cold old age came creeping on.*

Such thoughts, as Masefield showed in his poem, soften a hard man for penitence, and bring him face to face with God.

Saul had been called to a high task and a noble enterprise. He lost the vision of it in self-will, arrogance and disobedience. He wasted his energies on hate. He was unable to keep his word. He was blessed with noble friends; Samuel who had once loved him, David who had sought to serve him, Jonathan his own son. He was unable to give himself to their affection, their guidance and their consistent loyalty.

To be sure there was a streak of madness in the man, but his mental disorder was fed by what he wilfully entertained in his heart. We become that which we choose to be in a very real way. Hold hate at the core of the being and it eats up the personality, until none can encounter the host without a confrontation with the evil which has come to dwell within him. The same is true of love, of Christ in the heart. That is why it should be life's chief concern how 'each goes out at journey's end'.

62 : The Amalekite
2 Samuel 1.1–16

David was back two days from his punitive campaign against the Amalekites. Had his tough fighting-force been with Saul, the disaster of Mount Gilboa might not have occurred, but it was not David's fault that his hardened warriors had no part in Saul's army.

He was camping in the ruins of Ziklag when a lone Amalekite came down the mountain trails, either making for home or, a less likely suggestion, seeking David, with advantage for himself in mind. The true account of Saul's death is found in the previous chapter. The Amalekite was a liar. He had no doubt been haunting the area of battle like a jackal, in order to strip the dead, or to pick up some useful weapons and armour. His encounter with David, himself just back from scattering and punishing his desert tribesmen, was perhaps the last meeting he desired. His quick-witted and most circumstantial lying was both his attempt to extricate himself from a perilous situation, and to secure the reward which, by the base standards of his own depraved people, would have certainly been forthcoming. Rent clothes and hair befouled was the adjustment of a moment.

It was ironical that an Amalekite should tell this story, after both Saul's and David's relations with that people. David was hardly likely to overlook a crime against the man whom he himself had twice spared in reverence for the unction of God which had once lain on him, and the liar paid the penalty for the death he had professed to deal. Crude evil overreached itself.

'A lie is troublesome,' wrote Joseph Addison, 'and sets a man's invention upon the rack, and one trick needs a great many to make it good. It is like building upon a false foundation which continually stands in need of props to shore it up.' The Amalekite had been at his scavenger's task in the night before the Philistines found Saul's body. He had looted crown and bracelet. The theft led to the invention, itself twisted to win an ignoble end, and complicated by the mistake so often made by vicious men—that of imagining that others are like themselves. Simon the sorcerer thought he could secure the benison of the Holy Spirit from the apostles for money. Such propositions add crudity to vice.

Questions and themes for study and discussion on Studies 57–62

1. 'Reputation, reputation . . . O, I have lost my reputation. I have lost the immortal part of me, and what remains is bestial' (*Othello*). In what sense is this true of Nabal? Why is reputation of value?

2. Courtesy in the New Testament.

3. The Christian in worldly society. What rules govern participation?

4. Compromise, its cause and cure.

5. 'It is not the beginning of an enterprise but the ending thereof which bringeth true glory' (Drake).

6. Lying. What is the danger contained in the habit? See last paragraph of Study 61.

THE HOLY TRINITY

Plurality in Unity (New Testament Epistles)

63 : The Spirit and Christ
2 Corinthians 3.12–18

This is the close of a wonderful passage (2 Cor. 3.4–18) in which the glory of the new covenant in Christ is set over against the lesser glory of the old Mosaic covenant. It contains problems of interpretation. The most important key to these problems is in the hands of the reader, however, when he sees that Paul's mind is dwelling upon Exod. 34.29–35.

The chief problem is the way in which he appears to identify Christ and the Spirit in v. 17. This is a difficulty, because Paul normally treats them as distinct Persons, although our experience of them is one. The Exodus passage describes Moses before the people, and Moses before the Lord. Before the people (except when actually delivering God's commandments to them) Moses wore a veil over his face, but when he went in again to the presence of God he removed it. These times in the presence of God left their mark on his face, but the glow there gradually faded while it was being covered by the veil (2 Cor. 3.13) and it was not renewed until he was in the Divine presence once again.

All this, says Paul in effect, is a kind of parable of the situation today; the legalistic Jewish descendants of Moses, reading the old covenant, which came through him, find his writings just as impossible to discern as his face had been then when the veil covered it (14 f.). But when—like him—they turned to the Lord, the veil was removed (16). So the unconverted Jew is being likened to Moses' hearers and the converted Jew to Moses himself.

Now 'the Lord is the Spirit'—i.e. 'the Lord' in the Exodus typology and therefore also in v. 16 is to be understood as the Spirit, that is, the Spirit of the Lord. It is certainly not usual for Paul to speak of conversion as a turning to the Spirit but this is more appropriate in this passage than perhaps anywhere else, for he has been emphasizing (2 Cor. 3.3, 6, 8) the essential spirituality of the new covenant in contrast to Jewish legalism, and this spirituality is the product of the Spirit of God. He moves straight from the Spirit to Christ in v. 18, however.

Meditate on this verse, in the light of Exod. 34, and ask God to show you through it the secret of likeness to Christ.

54 : The Pre-eminence of Christ

Colossians 1.11-23

The Christians at Colosse were troubled by a heresy which, among other things, removed Christ from His throne and treated Him as just one of a series of mediators between God and men (2.18 f.). This kind of teaching is with us still. Paul exalts Christ throughout the whole epistle but nowhere in more exalted language than in this passage. Verses 15-20 have sometimes been considered a pre-Pauline hymn which Paul has incorporated within his epistle. Whether this be so or not, the passage comes to us with the stamp of Paul's apostolic authority upon it as does everything else in his letters.

Verses 11-14 make a bridge between the prayer which begins in v. 9 and the great doctrinal section which begins in v. 15. Verses 15-17 speak of His supremacy in the old creation and vs. 18-20 in the new. God cannot be seen by men but His Son has made Him known to us (15; cf. John 1.18; 14.9), for He, more than Adam could ever be, is the perfect Image of God. He is not just another Adam, however. He is far more, for as the 'firstborn of all creation' (15) He existed before Adam was created.

This expression is another which caused great debate during the Arian controversy (see Study No. 33). The Arians declared it taught that Christ is a creature. This cannot be, however, for v. 16 tells us that 'in him all things were created' and so He stands apart from all creatures. Rather, we should understand an allusion to the position of the firstborn in the Old Testament society. He was the father's chief heir and in his absence had authority over his brothers and sisters. This authority was an earnest of that headship over the family which was to be his in due course. The Messianic King is called 'firstborn' in a passage which emphasizes His supremacy (Psa. **89**.27). So Christ is supreme over the universe, and is the Agent of its creation. He is also its End ('for him', 16) and the One who holds it together (17).

His supremacy in the new creation is just as absolute; He is not only the Head of all angelic and supernatural beings (16, cf. **2**.10) but also of His new-created Church, having established His position by resurrection triumph (18). Note the twofold use of the term 'firstborn' (15, 18), and other parallels between the two sections of the passage. His pre-eminence in everything (18), whether the old or the new, is grounded in His absolute deity (19). He is no creature but the very incarnation of God. Lest our thought should become too abstract Paul moves on (20–23) to a reminder that this great One has put us for ever in His debt by His reconciling death. This gives the Christian's worship a constant note of thanksgiving.

65 : Son, God, Lord

Hebrews 1.1–2.4

The opening of the Letter to the Hebrews is deeply impressive. The author has a distinctive theme to expound—the high priesthood of Jesus Christ—but he begins on the highest possible note by expounding His deity. He differs from the prophets, not in bringing truth to men (for they did that also), but because His disclosure is complete and final (**1**.1 f.), for He is Son of God.

'He reflects the glory of God' and 'bears the very stamp of his nature.' The first of these assertions emphasizes His oneness in nature with the Father, just as the sun's rays are one with the sun itself: 'Light of Light, very God of very God.' The second uses the analogy of a die or seal: He the exact 'Counterpart of the Father'. Col. 1 (cf. Study No. 64) attributed both the creation and the upholding of the universe to Him. So does this letter (1.2 f.).

Heb. 1.5–14 consists of a series of seven quotations. The very number perhaps symbolizes the perfection of the Old Testament witness to Christ. Great titles appear in them. 'Son', 'God', 'Lord'—no title can be too exalted to apply to Him. The quotation from Psa. 102 (1.10–12) is particularly impressive. Look at its context in the psalm. It shows no evidence of being Messianic and yet the writer to the Hebrews applies it without argument to Jesus. The words of the psalm are addressed to God, and so both the writer and his readers clearly believed that Christ is God.

Throughout the whole of our passage we are made aware of the superiority of the Saviour to angels. If He is greater than they, the revelation through Him must be received and obeyed (2.1–4). He has already been called 'Lord' (1.10). Now this exalted title (used regularly in the Septuagint—the Greek version of the Old Testament—to translate the great Name, Yahweh) is used again (2.3).

Heb. 2.3 f. is a Trinitarian passage, for it brings together the three Persons in the work of salvation. We shall find this over and over again in the remaining studies. It is in connection with His purpose of redemption that God shows us His triunity. There could not be a more wonderful context for such a revelation!

> 'Join all the glorious names of wisdom, love, and
>   power,
> That ever mortals knew, that angels ever bore :
> All are too mean to speak His worth,
> Too mean to set my Saviour forth.'
>
> (Isaac Watts.)

66 : 'In the Son and in the Father'

1 John 2.24–3.8

Readers familiar with the AV (KJV) will note that the RSV omits the words of 1 John 5.7 ('For there are three that bear record in heaven, the Father, the Word, and the Holy Ghost, and these three are one.') These words are rightly omitted. The ancient manuscript evidence establishes beyond reasonable doubt that they are not part of the original text of 1 John. If we accept the full inspiration of Scripture it is important for us to receive only what the evidence shows to have been part of the original. Only a small fragment of the biblical evidence for the Trinity is thus removed, however.

The readers of this letter were familiar with the heresy of Cerinthus, who distinguished the man Jesus from the heavenly Christ who descended upon him at his baptism and left him before his death. John's approach to this matter in his teaching clearly reveals his Trinitarianism. If his readers continue to be true to the apostolic teaching ('what you heard from the beginning', 2.24), then they will abide in the Son and in the Father. This shows that it is equally valid to describe a true Christian as abiding in the Son or in the Father (cf. 2.22 f.). John's statement testifies eloquently to his belief in the deity of Jesus and His equality with the Father, and this becomes even clearer when he says, 'abide in him' (2.28) without specifying which Person is in view.

Indeed, a careful study of 2.28–3.7 will reveal a number of places where it is by no means certain whether John is writing of the Father or the Son. References to the second advent (2.28; 3.2) and to the atonement (3.5) certainly point to the Son, but the easy way in which John passes from the Father to the Son in his thought without indicating that he is doing so gives us a glimpse into a mind in which the two Persons were so intimately linked that to distinguish between them in his writing was not always of paramount importance. He also refers obliquely to the Spirit in 2.27 (cf. 2.20; 2 Cor 1.21 f.). The Spirit gives the Christian an instinct for the truth (cf. 5.7).

Meditation : Christ in the Father, Christ in the word, Chris. in the heart.

Questions and themes for study and discussion on Studies 63–6

1. What is the place of the Holy Spirit in making us like Christ?

2. How can the pre-eminence of Christ find practical expression in my life today?

3. Why should the letter to the Hebrews, which is chiefly concerned with the *work* of Christ, open with such an impressive passage on His *person*?

4. How is it that heresy concerning Christ or the Trinity undermines the whole Christian faith?

CHARACTER STUDIES

67 : David's Lament

2 Samuel 1.17–27; 1 Corinthians 13

It was the habit of David to turn the experiences of life into lyric poetry. Such poems, addressed to God, formed his psalms. This lament for the fallen does not quite fall into the category. It is not a prayer, nor specifically directed towards God, but it shows David's poetic power at its best.

It also reveals his character. Many versions retain the RV rendering which calls this poem 'the Song of the Bow'. The reason for the title would seem to be David's tender recollection of one of the last meetings with his friend, when Jonathan feigned archery practice to come to him secretly outside the town. The word 'bow' occurs in v. 22, a key line of the song.

It shows the deep strain of generosity in the singer. He ordered the learning of the song throughout all Israel. He was no small, mean-spirited man who feared the reputation of any predecessors. Jonathan might worthily have held the kingship. Saul had qualities which, as the men of Jabesh-Gilead had just movingly demonstrated, some folk vividly remembered.

David writes no 'taunt-song', no lyric of personal triumph. There is no sour note of denunciation for the dead, nor any recollection of evil or suffering. Saul was God's anointed, and David could never forget that this carried some seal of divine calling. Hence the notes of praise for the unfortunate man.

The attitude was no act of calculated policy. David had demonstrated enough the grace which determined his forgiving spirit towards his persecutor. At the same time, such libera magnanimity was likely to help solve the divisions of the land. David was about to found afresh a unified monarchy, and division might well find origin in a continuing rift between those who followed David and those who remembered Saul.

David, too, had a strong capacity for friendship. His love for Jonathan vibrates through his verse. So, too, does his patriotism. The death of Saul is to David no elimination of a personal foe, but a blow against the country over which the pagan foe might well indulge his ungodly glee. There is no reproach in patriotism. One who has not risen to the level of clean and simple patriotism is not likely to rise to the levels which other virtues demand.

68 : David's Summary

Psalm 18

Gratitude overwhelmed David when he looked back over the decade of his sufferings, and saw how worthwhile all his trials had been. David had learned vital lessons. He had proved the faithfulness of God. In crowded imagery (2), such as that found in Pss. 31 and 71, he extols the protection God had given him. He had seen the wild storm break over the Judean ranges (7–16), and thought how like the tempests of life the violence of Nature was . . . God keeps His promises (30). He gives strength (32, 39). He answers prayer (35).

After trial and tribulation, David could declare that life was worth the living. What is life? Man's life is warfare, said Job; 'a long fool's errand to the grave,' said Housman. 'Draw the curtain,' said dying Rabelais, 'the farce is played out.' 'Life is real, and life is earnest,' said Longfellow, who had suffered intensely, 'and the grave is not its goal.'

This psalm is David's answer, and the answer is very close to that of Paul: 'For me to live is Christ.' Amid calamitous events, betrayal, treachery, exile in the wilderness, frustration, misrepresentation and malice, David found a song to sing. If God was over all, permitting no suffering that He was not able to turn to usefulness, allowing no defeat which He was not certain to transmute into His own form of victory, then life was gladness, confidence, jubilant adventure. Even failure,

99

backsliding and stumbling are not outside such transformation.

The outburst of the heart in the first words of the psalm shows David to be one with those who knew God in Christ, rather than in company with the judges and the men of dim and stumbling faith who had filled the annals of the preceding century. Such was the conclusion to which David came, on some quiet evening, perhaps in Hebron, as he looked back over the tumultuous years. They were to prove the greatest years of his life.

It is good thus to look back and trace the path of guidance. But life, as Kierkegaard said, 'though it can be only understood backwards must be lived forward.' There can be no pausing. 'Hitherto the Lord has helped us' (1 Sam. 7.12), is a stand of faith only when it is the basis of new committal and daily dedication. He gives His marching orders day by day.

69 : David Crowned

2 Samuel 2.1–7; Psalm 101

Much had been taken from David's path by the death of Saul. He sought counsel of God (1), and was sent up to Hebron, one of the ancient cities of the land. There Abraham had pitched his tent in the oak woods, there he had bought Sarah's burying-place. The place was tangled with history for a thousand years before David made it his first royal seat.

It is possible that Psa. 101 was his self-imposed charter of royalty at this momentous juncture of his life. He begins with an ideal of blameless conduct (2), using the same verb as is used in 1 Sam. 18.14 f., where David 'had success'. He is picking up the theme of Psa. 15, so that blameless conduct may reasonably be said to be the consistent objective of his life. It is sad to think that the bright ideal was to be so savagely assailed. The early years of his reign were, at any rate, beyond reproach.

Call the psalm, as one commentator does, 'the Moral Ideals of a King,' and observe the qualities he covets and the vices he abhors. The first is 'integrity of heart' (see Psa. 78.72), ex-

plained by the next clause. The refusal to contemplate baseness fortifies the personality against evil. Integrity means
absence of corruption, that completeness which God would
have in His people.

Nor will he have the shallow and the apostate around him
(3). He seeks steadfastness, a word we have already examined.
'Perverseness of heart' (4) means obstinate resistance to good,
the dedication to evil which Christ found damnable in the
Pharisees. Nor will he have liars and slanderers or arrogant
men around him. We have seen how acutely David suffered
in soul and in circumstances from such vicious foes. He
swears to destroy them (5).

He wants faithful men about him (6), men at whose conduct none shall point reproach, no liars (7), no evildoers (8).
The phrase 'morning by morning' refers, of course, to the
Oriental royal custom of the matutinal audience (2 Sam.
15.2). Little by little he purposed to eliminate bad men from
the land. It was a grand ideal which the thirty-year-old
(2 Sam. **5**.4) king set himself. He desired a pure land, as the
writer of Psa. **104** desired a pure earth. The accomplishment
has eluded good rulers of all ages but finds its last apoca-
lyptic expression in Rev. **21**.27—'Nothing unclean shall enter
it, nor anyone who practises abomination or falsehood.'

70 : The Soldiers

2 Samuel 2.12–32; 3.12–39

Saul was naturally popular in Gilead, and his marshal, Abner,
an opportunist and a foe of David, took the opportunity to
frustrate the Hebron régime and its hopes of national unity
by setting up Saul's son as king at Mahanaim. Judah alone
was loyal to David. The rest of the land was divided—
bewildered by conflicting loyalties, or desperately following
Abner's puppet. It was unlikely that a trans-Jordanian government could hold wide sway in territories west of the great
valley. Nor was it likely that David was without support in
Mahanaim. Some of his guerrilla activities had been based
there, and a score of years later he found a safe refuge and
support at Mahanaim when he retreated before Absalom.

Abner was a soldier of the worst type, accustomed to war
and bloodshed, careless of the land's peace, a militarist who

saw his way of life at an army's head and in troubled times. War did not brutalize David. Like Jephthah, who was curiously enlightened at this one point, he preferred the ways of peace. The High Command, the General Staff, and other groups exploiting military power, sometimes force the hand of governments.

This note is written as 1970 ends. In 1870, one century ago, Bismarck's editing of the Ems telegram began the series of events which ran on to 1914, 1939, and the tensions of today. The pressure of the oiled and efficient Prussian war machine was a factor in precipitating the war with France, which sparked the long hatred of Germany and her neighbour. The war-clouds were receding when Bismarck played his unscrupulous hand. The army chief, Helmut von Moltke, said Bismarck in his memoirs, looked 'quite old and frail,' when he thought the war with France was not going to break out. He took the 'old bloodletter', as he described him, to a table, and showed him how the abbreviation and distortion of the famous telegram would make war quite inevitable. Moltke looked quite spry and fresh again, when sure of the war, which was his trade. He showed how the soul can die.

Such a man was Abner, ready to cry peace when his cause collapsed (2.26), ready to change sides at need (3.12), and dying as he had lived. Joab, who killed him, was no better. He was David's nephew, and David's marshal, but a thorn in David's side.

71 : Ishbosheth

2 Samuel 4

Eshbaal was probably the real name of Saul's unfortunate son (1 Chron. 8.33; 9.39). During the period of the judges and on into the monarchy many names were compounded with 'baal', a word which means 'master', and could apply to Israel's God. It was the introduction of Phoenician idolatry, and the growing problem of the fertility cults (Hos. 2.16), which gave the name its pagan connotations, and banished it from nomenclature. Hence the substitution in retrospect, in this man's name, of 'bosheth' which means 'shame'. Ishbosheth was the 'man of shame'.

There are those in history and in life who are caught up in some catastrophic stream of events and driven to a fate not of their own making. Perhaps Pilate was one, but Pilate was able at any moment to break out of the encompassing tangle of circumstances by one heroic, if costly, act of will. Perhaps the pathetic Ishbosheth could have done the same. The record is brief, and has nothing to say of those conversations or compulsions by which Abner forced the prince's hand. He was forty years of age, no romantic, inexperienced youth. He had watched with adult eyes the development of his own father's tragedy. He must have talked with his brother Jonathan, whose eyes were open to the shape of coming events.

Perhaps he was a legalist, who stood upon what he considered the letter of the law, his right of succession. Curiously enough, Nelson Glueck, rabbi, historian and archaeologist, still stands by Ishbosheth's legal right, and, describing the Jabbok gorge, pictures David in hazardous retreat from Absalom up its wild course. Almost in the spirit of a Hebrew taunt-song, he writes: 'What thoughts weigh down the weary shoulders of this refugee? No Nathan is necessary this time to accuse him of having stolen the poor man's only ewe lamb. The rushing stream, the stabbing thorns, the frowning hills shout insistently, "The sin is thine, O David, and vengeance is the Lord's." Dark forebodings tugged at his heart strings.'

But David had nothing on his conscience concerning Ishbosheth. He avenged his murder. There was no right of absolute succession in the young monarchy. David was called of God to the kingship, and Jonathan, the eldest son of Saul, had recognized the fact. Nor would the weak and shadowy Ishbosheth have been other than Abner's tool in a new round of war, division and tension.

Questions and themes for study and discussion on Studies 67–71

1. Why is patriotism out of fashion in some quarters today?

2. Perversity of heart. Define and consider.

3. Integrity. Define and illustrate.

4. Past, present and future in Christian experience.

5. Need anyone be used by bad men?

THE HOLY TRINITY

Three in One (Part 1)

72 : The Trinity and the Baptism

Mark 1.1–11

The Gospel of Mark was written for Romans. It portrays
Jesus Christ as 'the Son of God' (1). We often tend to think
of the Fourth Gospel as that of His Sonship, but the Second
also emphasizes it (cf. 1.11; 3.11; 5.7; 9.7; 12.6; 13.32; 14.61 f.;
15.39). This title shows His transcendence and His relationship to God. Even 13.32, which for many constitutes a problem but which bears testimony to the reality of our Lord's
humanity, shows His greatness, for it places His knowledge
above that of all men and even of angels.

We have already commented on vs. 2 f. in the study on
Mal. 3 (Study No. 45). John the Baptist, said by our Lord to
be the greatest among those born of women (Matt. 11.11),
speaks here of his utter personal unworthiness and of the
inferiority of his work to that of Jesus (7 f.).

For our purposes perhaps the most important aspect of this
passage is the association of the three Persons at the baptism
of our Lord. In the third century the heresy of modalism
found its most prominent representative in Sabellius. He
maintained that the three Persons are not eternal distinctions
within the one life of God but consecutive manifestations, the
Father in the Old Testament, the Son in the Gospels, and the
Holy Spirit from Pentecost onwards. When God began to
manifest Himself as the Son, He ceased to manifest Himself
as the Father, and so on. Believers of the time had many

objections to this doctrine but the 'baptism of our Lord' was perhaps the simplest answer. No attempt to deal with the biblical evidence which does not result in an acceptance of the eternity and deity of the three Persons can be substantiated. This is a great mystery but it is not open to us to adjust the Bible's teaching to our own preconceptions.

> '*Almighty God, to Thee be endless honours done,*
> *The undivided Three, and the mysterious One.*
> *Where reason fails, with all her powers,*
> *There faith prevails and love adores.*'
>
> (*Isaac Watts*)

73 : Indwelt by the Triune God
John 14.15–31; 15.26, 27

The Upper Room discourse is rich with material bearing on the doctrine of the Trinity. Our Lord was dealing there with truths which would be of particular importance to His disciples in the future.

At Pentecost the Holy Spirit, who was no Stranger to them (**14.**17), would come to indwell them and to be with the Church for ever (**14.**16 f.). There have been attempts from time to time to deny the personality and the Deity of the Spirit. The expression 'another Counsellor' (**14.**16) establishes both facts, however. The term 'spirit' is neuter in Greek, but this is purely a grammatical matter, of no more significance than the fact that the Greek word for 'child' is also neuter! But the word translated 'Counsellor' (whatever may be its best rendering) describes the office of a person. It could not conceivably be used of a mere impersonal influence or power. Greek possesses two words which could be translated into English as 'another', one really meaning 'another of the same sort' and the other 'another of a different sort'. It is the first of these which is employed here. If Jesus is Lord of all, and the Holy Spirit takes His place, surely He too must be a Divine Person!

The Spirit is sent by the Father in Christ's name (**14.**26), and so He is intimately related to both. In **15.**26 He is said to proceed from the Father. The early Fathers used to speak of the 'eternal generation' of Christ and the 'procession' of the Spirit from the Father. The first term is an attempt to express the idea that Christ is Son of God and yet is eternal. The second seeks to relate the Spirit to the Father in a similar way without saying that He too is Son, for the Bible does not allow us to say this of Him. If the Son and the Spirit are God, they must be eternal, but it seems unlikely that the words of 15.26 look beyond the historical gift of the Spirit at Pentecost.

14.23 gives us an amazing statement. Who is this that joins Himself with the Father and says '*We* will come'? Yet, just a few verses later He says, 'the Father is greater than I' (14.28). This reminds us that the incarnation did not rob Him of His deity but did involve His true humanity, and so a voluntary subjection to the Father (31, cf. Phil. 2.5–11).

74 : 'Jesus of Nazareth . . . Lord of all'

Acts 10.30–43

The Acts of the Apostles records for us the first Christian sermons. One of the most interesting of these is Peter's message to Cornelius and his friends. It has been noted that it is almost like a summary of the Gospel of Mark, which, like the sermon, commences its unfolding of the good news (36, cf. Mark 1.1) with the ministry of John the Baptist (37; Mark 1.4–8).

Like all the apostolic sermons in the Acts it exultantly proclaims the fact of our Lord's resurrection (39–41) and declares Jesus to be 'Lord' (36). As we have noticed in an earlier study (No. 65), the Greek word '*kyrios*', translated 'Lord' in the New Testament, is employed in the Septuagint (the Greek version of the Old Testament) to translate the great name of God, Yahweh. This is of special importance, for Luke was a Greek Christian with a knowledge of the Septuagint and he would be well aware of the significance of such a term when used among people who knew the Old Testament. Remember that Cornelius was 'a devout man' (10.2), which would mean that he was a Gentile frequenter of the synagogue and so would be acquainted with the Old Testament. The fact that in Peter's sermon here Jesus is not only called 'Lord' but 'Lord of all' (36), cannot possibly mean anything less than full deity.

Verse 38 is Trinitarian in form and reminds us of the association of the three holy Persons at the baptism of our Lord (cf. Study No. 72). In his own Gospel Luke shows us the work of the Spirit in the ministry of Jesus (Luke 3.22; 4.1, 14, 18, etc.); during His ministry He was led by the Spirit (Luke 4.1), while after His resurrection He sent the Spirit (Acts 2.33). And, it should be noted, God was behind the ministry of both Jesus and the Holy Spirit (38, cf. Gal. 4.4–6).

A thought : The command of God (42) stands for us too (Matt. 28.18–20).

75 : 'The Spirit of life in Christ Jesus'

Romans 8.1–11

The letter to the Romans is usually regarded as Paul's *magnum opus.* One who knew the other Pauline letters but not Romans might find it surprising that there are so few references to the Holy Spirit in the first seven chapters. 1.4 and 5.5 are the only two, and some commentators question whether the first of these concerns the Third Person of the Trinity. Whether or not Paul has refrained deliberately from much reference to Him, it is certain that this makes the fullness of reference to Him in ch. 8 all the more impressive.

Chapter 7 has revealed the inability of a Christian man to live the Christian life victoriously on the basis simply of the new motivation which conversion gives (7.13–25). He needs a new power also, and this too is supplied by God through the Spirit. Not surprisingly, it is the Spirit's work which is chiefly in view here, but there are some important verses which throw light upon His Person (9–11). What is so interesting in Rom. 8 is the fact that Paul gives us a series of terms which seem to be virtual equivalents: 'the Spirit', 'the Spirit of God', 'the Spirit of Christ', 'Christ', 'the Spirit of him who raised Jesus from the dead', 'his Spirit'. These titles provide us with a clear indication of the intimate relationship between the Spirit and God and Christ. The same Person can be referred to, apparently indifferently, as 'the Spirit of God' and 'the Spirit of Christ'.

The term we do not expect here is 'Christ'. Is Paul identifying the Son and the Spirit? No! The whole passage is about the work of God in the inner life of the believer. The same *experience* can be validly described now in terms of Christ in us, and now in terms of the Spirit in us. The Spirit is God at work in the inner life but He works in order to impart to us the life of Christ and to conform us to His image. What he is saying, then, when put in terms of later theology, is that Christ indwells us by His Spirit (cf. v. 2).

A question. If the Spirit who indwells me is really the Spirit of Christ who indwelt Him during the days of His flesh, what kind of qualities does He seek to produce in my life?

76 : Knowing God through His Spirit

1 Corinthians 2

All the Greeks prized wisdom and the Corinthians were no exception. As so often happens, the Corinthian Christians were affected by the intellectual atmosphere in which they lived. The desire for wisdom engendered pride and was a chief cause of the divisions which appeared among them. Paul spends much of ch. 1 in setting things in their right perspective. He shows that God's revelation and salvation cut right across human ways of thinking.

In ch. 2 he declares that his own preaching was not with a show of wisdom but in the power of the Spirit (1–5). He then goes on to speak positively about wisdom, for God has His own wisdom which He has willed to impart and which has already been defined as Christ (6–8, cf. 1.24, 30). The Divine wisdom is revealed to us through the Spirit (9–13), and this is why the ungodly man cannot understand spiritual truth (14–16).

For our purpose vs. 10 f. are of considerable importance. The Lord Jesus declared (Matt. 11.25–27) the mutual knowledge of the Father and the Son, and now Paul declares the power also of the Spirit to penetrate to the depths of God. Why can He do this? Because, says Paul in effect, He sustains the same kind of relationship to God as a man's spirit does to the man himself. B. B. Warfield well sums up the implications of this: 'Here the Spirit appears . . . as the principle of God's knowledge of Himself: He is, in a word, just God Himself in the innermost essence of His Being. As the spirit of man is the seat of human life, the very life of man itself, so the Spirit of God is His very life-element.' Moreover the Spirit is intimate with Christ also, for Christ is God, and so through the Spirit 'we have the mind of Christ' (16).

> *'Come, Holy Ghost . . .*
> *God, through Himself, we then shall know if Thou*
> *within us shine,*
> *And sound, with all Thy saints below, the depths of*
> *love divine.'*
>
> *(Charles Wesley)*

77 : Diversity in Unity

1 Corinthians 12.1–13

The title of this study may be equally applied to the main theme of 1 Cor. 12, the gifts of the Spirit (1), or else to the three Persons referred to in vs. 4–6. It may be that somebody in the Corinthian church had cried out in a state of ecstasy 'Jesus be cursed!' The function of the Holy Spirit is always to glorify the Lord Jesus, and so Paul declares that such utterances are clearly not of the Spirit.

This is one important principle. Another is that the many diverse gifts given by the Spirit to individual believers are all intended for the good of the whole church. Almost the entire chapter is devoted to an exposition of this. It is in this connection that Paul makes the important statement of vs. 4–6. Each Person of the Trinity has His own distinctive functions in the work of salvation. The Father plans it, the Son executes it and the Spirit administers it. It is the Spirit to whom is normally attributed the spiritual gifts operative in the church, but the apostle finds no difficulty in attributing them also to Christ ('the same Lord') or the Father ('the same God'). Many theologians have made use of the idea of the 'coinherence' of the divine Persons. Because they are most intimately related, the works of One may often be attributed to Another. Indeed, to quote Augustine, 'as They are inseparable, so They operate inseparably.'

A thought. If the Spirit of God dwells in me He will never lead me to do anything which draws attention to myself and away from Christ.

78 : 'Grace . . . love . . . fellowship'
2 Corinthians 13

This chapter has been included in the studies because of the verse with which it closes, but you should seek to profit also by the rest of it. Paul has had to write some stern things to the Corinthians in this letter. He hopes that his words of warning will make it unnecessary for him to come to them as a strong disciplinarian later on. All his ministry was for the 'improvement' (9) or 'building up' (10) of the people of God and he still ministers to us in this way through his letters.

The words of the 'grace' (14) are striking not only for the association of the Three Persons as Sources of blessing for men. Paul often links the Father and the Son in this kind of way, as he does at the start of this very letter (1.2). His inclusion of the Spirit in this type of passage is not so frequent. Still more striking, however, is the order in which they are mentioned. We are used to referring to the Father, Son and Spirit as the First, Second and Third Persons of the Trinity. This use of terms is not inappropriate, for in the great plan of redemption the Father sent the Son and the Spirit (Gal. 4.4–6), and the Son also sends the Spirit (John 15.26). Yet it should not make us forget that the Three are equal in power and glory. It is this truth that the variation of order from time to time helps to safeguard. The order here is really that of experience. 'There can be no adequate understanding of God's love apart from the cross; and the only lasting fellowship between men is the fellowship of sinners redeemed by the blood of Jesus' (R. V. G. Tasker).

These words of Paul employed in Christian worship more frequently than any others, except perhaps those of the Lord's Prayer, furnish a constant reminder to Christians of the Trinitarian nature of the God they worship and whom they have been brought to know.

Questions and themes for study and discussion on Studies 72–78

1. What other evidence would you bring to refute the views of Sabellius (Study No. 72)?

2. From John **14–16** gather material showing what was to be the relationship of the disciples to the Father, to the Son and to the Spirit.

3. Cornelius believed in God before he became a Christian, and could well have been a believer in an Old Testament sense, like Abraham and others. How would the acceptance of Christ and the indwelling of the Spirit of Christ enrich his experience of God?

4. A survey of different translations of Rom. **8**.1–6 will show that there is no general agreement among translators as to whether Paul is writing here of the Spirit of God or the spirit of believers. Does it matter?

5. Compare 1 Cor. **2** with our Lord's teaching about the work of the Spirit in John **16**.12–15.

6. To what extent does Paul's teaching that the Spirit glorifies Christ and edifies the Church enable us to distinguish a genuine work of the Spirit from a counterfeit?

7. How appropriate is the common use of the words of 2 Cor. **13**.14 at the close of a service of Christian worship?

CHARACTER STUDIES

79 : David's Household

2 Samuel 3.1–6; 5

These events, briefly chronicled, and sometimes reaching back in time to resume a thread, may also be read in the Chronicles (e.g. 1 Chron. 11–14). Sometimes a relevant or interesting detail is added by the second narrative.

As we seek, however, to isolate the picture of David's person, and to understand his character, we can pass by the briefly told record of war, the capture of Jerusalem, and the renewed threat from the Philistines of the Gaza Strip. From the passages before us, one blemish on David's reign, the social reflection of a blemish in his character, springs out—his disordered and polygamous household.

It is a truth which can be abundantly illustrated from both literature and life, that good men can be blind to some aspects of evil. There were good Christians in the first century and in the nineteenth, who had no conscience about the evil and crime of slavery. Luther's writings abundantly illustrate the defectiveness of his social conscience in certain aspects of government and authority.

And David was a child of his age in matters of sex. The defect was to betray him twice, and lead to ruinous and agonizing sequences of events. The tensions and problems of the harem are obvious. No household is safe where polygamy forms a hotbed and breeding-ground for plot, counter-plot, and base intrigue. This was a legacy which David was to hand on to the brilliant Solomon, and which was to ruin his reign.

Was David responsible for this moral defect? David was a

man of deep insight into the mind of God. He was a man of understanding. He must have had misgivings. Moreover, he had before his eyes, knowing as he did the old history of his race, the example of the patriarchs. Abraham had one wife, and Abraham's one adventure in deviation, justified by Sumerian law though it was, produced disaster. Monogamy was implicit in the Creation story, and polygamy appeared first in the line of Cain. Through recorded history—Jacob, Moses, Gideon, and Elkanah, for example—trouble enough was generated in polygamous households. David had the information, the insight, and the intellect to know better. There was an unsanctified corner in his personality. Such a bridge-head of evil can be the source of inroads of catastrophe. Observe the process in the rest of David's story.

80 : David and the Ark

2 Samuel 6; Psalm 24

The strange story of David's bringing home the Ark of the Covenant should be read in the light of the triumph-song which celebrated its returning. The Ark was something more than a mere talisman, a sacred object, in David's mind, and this we learn only from the hymn which forms Psa. 24. Merely to read the story in the chronicler's account leaves the modern reader somewhat sympathetic towards Michal, who saw some despite to royal dignity and decency in David's ceremonial dancing before the Ark. He seems less than generous in his virtual divorce from her.

Psa. 24 reveals what was happening in heart and mind. To David the coming of the Ark to Jerusalem signified a return to pure worship. The lovely box containing the tablets of the Law, and, surmounted by the empty mercy-seat where the winged cherubim gazed down on abstract perfection, was a deeply significant object. Here was also a great historical event, and David sought to make the people to whom he had given a capital city, and now was giving a centre of divine worship, aware of Jehovah's greatness.

As the procession wound up the road to the citadel of Zion, the antiphonal singing of the Levitical choirs echoed round the rocky heights. God, the hymn proclaims, is no tribal totem (1 f.), but the ruler of the whole world and all the races in it. This was the vision of Abraham. It was to be the vision of Isaiah and of Paul. Nor could such a God be worshipped by the impure (3 f.). Observe again David's pre-occupation with candour, goodness, and love of truth. 'Clean hands' signifies righteousness in action and deed. The hands can be the tools of evil (Rom. 6.12 f.). They should be the servants of Christ (Rom. 12.1). A 'pure heart' signifies the desire for righteousness at the point of origin of all action—the centre of the personality.

The house of God is not an easy or a comfortable dwelling for those who have no desire for the One who reigns there (read C. S. Lewis' *Great Divorce*). The prerequisite of all blessing is not to 'lift up the soul to that which is false', those merchandise of Vanity Fair, the ephemeral, material objects of man's mistaken desires. Such are the children of God through all the ages—'those who seek Him'. And those who seek Him find blessing (Isa. 55.6–9).

But here, indeed, is insight into the personality of the writer. No other man, right to the threshold of his day, had such a penetrating insight into spiritual truth. The procession wound round the rocky track. The Ark, carried high on its stout poles (Exod. 25.10–22), passed through the gates. It was a great moment, spoiled, thought David, by proud Michal's sneer.

81 : David's Peace

2 Samuel 7

In human experience there is the valley of the shadow, and there are also, as David was to put it in a psalm, the still waters and the pleasant pastures. The embattled years were over, and the king lay in a patch of peace, and thought of God. There are those who call for help in the day of trouble, when the shadows are dark and the way perilous and rough. Then, with ease and prosperity, the heart, as Deuteronomy puts it (31.20), 'grows fat', and God is forgotten.

It is to David's honour that, when quietness came to his life, he thought of God and adornment for His worship. He sought to give God a worthy symbolic dwelling place, and the thought did him credit. We honour God still by worthy church buildings, for all the contrary notions of radical theologians. Nathan, who appears in the story for the first time, brought word that the gift was not to be, but also came with assurance of the continuity of David's house, a covenant to be strangely fulfilled in Christ.

David went in and 'sat before the Lord'. The phrase seems to occur nowhere else in Scripture, and betokens an intimacy in David's worship, a father and son relationship which prefigures the free entry of the Christian to the presence of his Lord (1 John 2.28). David prayed with heartfelt earnestness for the preservation of his line. It was a small desire seen in the perspective of God's larger plans. It was not answered on the plane on which David placed it, although a descendant of the son of Jesse did in truth sit upon Judah's throne for some four centuries.

It is the way of God to answer the heart's petitions (Psa. 37.4) on a level far beyond the fumbling words in which they are framed. We cannot know the future. God does. Our small wisdom cannot adequately define that which is best for us. God's wisdom is as complete and perfect as His love. 'His plans are not our plans', but His plans do not necessarily set our plans aside and frustrate them. God reinterprets, enlarges, sublimates and transforms. David would have prayed for a larger fulfilment, a more glorious kingdom, had he been able to conceive and to formulate the prayer. This was the answer given, and it was an answer built round the core of surrender and sincerity in the prayer the seeker prayed, as he sat before God in the dim shrine.

82 : David's Strife (1)

2 Samuel 8; Psalm 44

Much battling on the frontiers is compressed into this brief account. It is impossible to follow it in detail. It appears that major campaigns were undertaken in two directions, against Moab in the east, and against Aram or Syria in the north. The aim of the former thrust was iron. The Philistines, as we have seen, were men of the Iron Age. The Hebrews still lived in the Bronze Age. They lacked a vital weaponry. David sought the iron ores of Edom. Solomon was to build refineries near the Gulf of Aqaba. To the north, David sought a stable frontier, and the passing reference to Damascus suggests that at this time Israel reached its widest and most imperial boundaries.

The chronicler's bald account leaves out the gusts of anxiety, the days of tension and of stress, the weariness of conflict and all the tumult of war which David knew, over what may have been a considerable span of years. Thanks to the psalms, we may catch some echoes of his feelings and his prayers. Identification, in the absence of headings, must be conjectural, but it seems possible that Psa. 44 is Davidic, and belongs to this period, though to be sure some, including Calvin, have referred it to the time of the Maccabees.

Read it with these assumptions in mind. The first eight verses show the suppliant banking on his reserves of divine salvation. 'Our fathers have told us . . .' God who did great things in the past can act again. But in vs. 9–16 the mood changes. On such stormy frontiers, with the heathen raging (Psa. 2), it was not possible to live in the continual light of victory. There befell days of disaster, and the psalmist searches his heart and the ways of his people to discover the reason. He finds himself bearing the burden of the nation's backsliding and its sin, and in protestation and confession falls before God's holiness, and pleads for pardon.

The remainder of the psalm, which is almost unrelieved in its gloom, calls for God to bless those who have thus humbled themselves before Him. God is pleased with well-worn prayers. Today is as full of Him as was yesterday. God's mercies are not withdrawn. The prayer is in God's hands.

83 : David's Strife (2)

1 Chronicles 18; Psalm 60

Psa. 60 may certainly be referred to this period. The old rabbinical headings represent an ancient tradition, not to be lightly set aside. The psalm was written on the morrow of a defeat, followed by unexpected victory. It is not to be supposed that David's wide reorganization of the complicated frontiers of Israel proceeded without fluctuations of military fortune. Edom and Moab appear to have attacked while David confronted the Syrians or Aramaeans in the north. Joab, David's rough soldier nephew, by some manoeuvre turned the tide.

The first three verses show what should be done with defeat in any sphere of life. The facts should be faced. Two courses are open in any sort of failure or defeat. The beaten man can lie down and submit, or he can rise and refuse to accept the situation. See Mic. 7.8 f. Note the pronoun: '. . . until *He* pleads my cause.' And see Rom. 8.31–39, especially in Phillips' translation.

Failure is not final. Failure confessed can be a stepping stone, a challenge, a spur, a stimulus to success. We have seen in the course of these studies, many failures turned to success —most notably Moses' failure. We shall see Mark and Peter.

Verse 4 ends obscurely in the RSV, and other versions differ widely over the same closing words, which are possibly corrupt in the text. The major portion of the verse is, however, clear. 'Thou hast set up a banner for those who fear thee, to rally to it . . .' The banner, in the dust and confusion of the battlefield, showed where the king was. A rallying point held hard-pressed men from scattering in rout. And so, as David had found in the days of life's defeats, when he was hemmed in he made for God, and God's truth. Experience of battle had woven his imagery.

The thought is, and David never wavered here, that God is near, involved, able and willing to help. There is no need for Job's despairing 'Oh, that I knew where I might find him . . .' And look at the closing words of Isa. 54. Here then is a secret of the psalmist's life. He was often defeated. We shall soon read of his most shocking defeat. And we shall see him rally from that defeat, moving back to where the banner stood—and God, ready to hold the broken line and give fresh courage.

Questions and themes for study and discussion on Studies 79–83

1. Christian marriage, fidelity, and the so-called 'permissive society'.
2. The symbolism of the Ark.
3. 'Far more abundantly than all that we ask or think' (Eph. 3.20).
4. Is any failure final?

THE HOLY TRINITY

Three in One (Part 2)

84 : 'All the fullness of God'

Ephesians 3.14–4.6

Paul's inspired thought is at its most complex in the letter
to the Ephesians. He begins to pray in 1.15, eventually moves
away from prayer to theological statement (1.20), returns to
prayer (3.1 'for this reason'; cf. 1.15), moves off immediately
at a tangent and resumes his prayer at 3.14, completing it
at the close of the chapter. What a wonderful prayer it is,
for he seeks enlightenment (1.15–20) and experience (3.14–19)
for his readers, and all for the glory of God (3.20 f.)!

Father, Spirit and Son are all seen to be deeply involved
in the believer's experience of God (3.14–19). They are to be
discerned also in 'him', 'the power at work within us', and
'Christ Jesus' in 3.20 f. Paul seems almost unable to think
about our experience of God without moving along Trinitarian lines, as if these were altogether natural for him as
a Christian.

The three Persons appear in reverse order in 4.4–6. Verse 6
is especially interesting. Although it speaks of God the Father,
it says of Him that He is 'above all and through all and in all'.
This language itself is Trinitarian. It defines the relationship
of the Father to the Spirit and the Lord to whom reference
has already been made in the preceding verses. The Father
plans our salvation as the sovereign Ruler of all things ('above
all', cf. 1.11); He accomplishes it through Jesus Christ

('through all') and applies it by the Spirit who indwells all believers ('in all'). In this way the functions of the Persons and their relation to each other become clear. The Son and the Spirit clearly accepted a position of subordination to the Father for the salvation of men. A study of the Gospel of John would show how fully our Lord was aware of this (e.g. cf. John 6.37–40; 14.26).

Meditation : Much of this passage is a prayer. Consider how the Christian doctrine of the Trinity helps our devotional life.

85 : A Sure Saying

Titus 3.1–8

The doctrinal content of the Pastoral Epistles (1 and 2 Timothy and Titus) is considerable and is often neglected. The letter to Titus contains two wonderfully full statements of Christian doctrine (2.11–14; 3.4–7). The one contained in our present passage is as full for its length as anything in the rest of the New Testament. There is much here that reminds us of Eph. 2.1–10. Paul concludes this summary by declaring, 'the saying is sure'. This passage shows us so clearly that the ethics of the New Testament are dependent on its theology, for the moral exhortations of vs. 1 f. are grounded completely in the doctrine that follows. Grace, salvation, regeneration, justification, sonship, eternal life—all this is here. The three Persons are mentioned, in the order Father (4), Spirit (5), Son (6).

Of special interest is the use of the words 'our Saviour' both of God and of Christ. In the Old Testament God is called the Saviour of His people (e.g. Psa. 106.21; Isa. 43.3). Especially is it made clear that in the deepest sense the term is applicable to God alone (Isa. 43.11; 45.21; Hos. 13.4). To attribute salvation to Christ, therefore, is tantamount to attributing Deity to Him, especially in a passage where God Himself is called 'Saviour'. Indeed, in Titus 2.13 it is quite possible that the RSV text preserves the correct translation as against the marginal rendering, although the latter is not impossible. This would mean that the whole expression 'the appearing of the glory of our great God and Saviour Jesus Christ' refers to Christ. The Greek reads most naturally this way.

> *'Renewed by Thy Spirit, redeemed by Thy Son,*
> *Thy children revere Thee for all Thou hast done.'*
>
> *(Georeg Rawson)*

86 : The Trinity and Old Testament Scripture

Hebrews 10.5–18

Earlier in this volume we considered the great opening of this letter (Study No. 65). As the argument of the letter has unfolded the writer has shown us the superiority of Christ in realm after realm. Especially from the beginning of ch. 7, however, he has tended more and more to concentrate attention upon His priesthood and sacrifice. These are certainly in the centre of the picture in this passage. In vs. 1–10 he is thinking of the perfect sacrifice of Jesus in contrast to the imperfect sacrifices of the Old Testament order and in vs. 11–14 he relates this to the fact that He is also High Priest.

The quotation from Psa. 40.6–8 which appears in vs. 5–7 and in fragments also in vs. 8–10, speaks of the will of God (7, 10). The writer understands that Christ speaks in the psalm and he evidently believes that the will of God referred to is not only the ethical requirements of God which abide for all men, and therefore for Christ as man, but the will of God to 'sanctify' His people through Christ's sacrifice of Himself. This reminds us of Gethsemane. So our salvation is attributed to the will of God.

It is also attributed to the sacrifice of the Son, and this is made as 'a single sacrifice . . . for all time' (12). Why was this so effective when the animal sacrifices, although God-ordained, had proved defective (1–4)? Because of His perfect humanity, of course. We need to remember, however, that all that this epistle says about His work rests upon the great statements of the first two chapters, which reveal that the One who came to offer such a sacrifice was none other than God manifest in the flesh. The eternal value of His sacrifice is due to the eternal nature of Him who made it.

The Holy Spirit has many functions in our redemption. The one selected here is that of bearing witness to it through the utterances of the Old Testament prophets (15–18).

87 : The Triune God in our Salvation

1 Peter 1.1–12

The great opening of this epistle strikes a Trinitarian note
straightaway (2). It is interesting to notice how often in the
New Testament the word 'God' is qualified by the expression
'the Father' when Christ is mentioned in the context (e.g. cf.
1 Cor. 15.24; Phil. 2.11). This may well suggest the awareness
of the New Testament writers that Christ is rightly called
'God' also. It is the Son and the Spirit who work for our
salvation within human history, for the sanctifying Spirit
applies to me now the efficacy of the blood of Christ shed at
Calvary. It is the Father who planned it all in eternity.

In v. 3 the great expression 'the God and Father of our
Lord Jesus Christ' is employed (cf. Eph. 1.3; 2 Cor. 1.3).
Here we see both the humanity of Christ (for He is His God)
and His deity (for He is His Father, and our Lord always
used this term in a special way, as we saw in Study No. 55).

The two references to the Spirit are of considerable interest.
We might have expected them to be reversed, for the
expression 'the Spirit of Christ' (11) is never used in the
Old Testament but is in the New (Rom. 8.9; cf. Acts 16.7;
Gal. 4.6), while the term 'the Holy Spirit' is found in both
(in the Old Testament in Psa. 51.11; Isa. 63.10). Peter is particularly concerned to stress, however, that the testimony of
the prophets to Christ's sufferings and glory was Divine and
not merely human (cf. 2 Pet. 1.19–21). For this reason the
title 'Spirit of Christ' is particularly appropriate as suggesting
that the witness of the Spirit in the old and new economies
was one, for Christ was always its Subject (cf. Heb. 10.15;
John 15.26).

> 'Thrice holy: Father, Spirit, Son;
> Mysterious Godhead, Three in One,
> Before Thy throne we sinners bend,
> Grace, pardon, life to us extend.'
>
> (*Edward Cooper*)

88 : God Begins to Reveal His Plan

Revelation 1.1–7

Some Christians tend to treat the book of the Revelation as if it were the most important part of Scripture, while others practically ignore it. Both attitudes are unbalanced. We should come to it bearing in mind the promise to the reader (3) and seeking through it a fuller knowledge of Christ. There is certainly no book of the Bible which speaks more eloquently of Him.

'Grace' and 'peace' appear with great frequency in the greetings which open many of the New Testament letters and there is frequent reference to the Father and the Son. Only here (4 f.) is the Holy Spirit also mentioned, and so this passage has its special importance in the New Testament evidence for the doctrine of the Trinity.

God is called 'him who is and who was and who is to come'. This expression violates the normal rules of Greek grammar, but we should remember that language is the servant of thought and not its master. Greek is an inflected language (in which words change their form to express changes in tense, number, case, etc.) and by what he does here John preserves the Divine name from inflection. This may be a means of stressing the absoluteness and changelessness of God. The whole expression reminds us of Exod. 3.14.

The number 7 has important symbolical significance in Scripture and especially in this book. It suggests completion or perfection. So 'the seven spirits' represent the Holy Spirit, who speaks to the seven churches of Revelation and is 'single in nature . . . multiple in distribution' (A. M. Farrer). The Spirit in all His sevenfold fullness rests on the Messiah (Isa. 11.2 f.; Rev. 5.5 f.).

Christ is probably placed last because John is going to write more fully of Him. Just as God is He 'who is and who was and who is to come', so Jesus Christ is 'the faithful witness' (probably a reference to His earthly ministry), 'the firstborn of the dead' (His resurrection), and 'the ruler of the kings of the earth' (His exaltation). This shows John's interest in the fulfilment of the purposes of God in history. Verses 5b–7 also point us to what He has done for us, what He will do in the future, and to the love which is our constant spiritual environment.

89 : The Son of Man in Majesty

Revelation 1.8–20

This passage is a continuation of the previous one and its chief feature is a vision of Christ in all His majesty. When John received this vision he was in a Spirit-initiated state of prophetic trance (10; cf. 4.2). It was therefore the Spirit of God who communicated this vision to him. This is further evidence of the Spirit's work of glorifying the Lord Jesus.

A study of Daniel 7 will reveal a rather remarkable fact. The language of John's vision owes much to that chapter and it contains elements from the prophet's vision both of the 'one like unto a son of man' and also of 'the Ancient of Days', clearly a title for God (cf. also Ezek. 1.24). This can only mean that John was made aware of the deity of the Son of Man. The whole vision and John's reaction to it (17) make us aware of the transcendent glory and dignity of the One described.

The exalted Lord laid His hand upon John. His words to him added further confirmation of His Divine nature (17 f.). He declared Himself to be the first and the last. This expression is drawn from Isa. 44.6 and 48.12 and in both the context makes it clear that the One who speaks is the only God and will tolerate no rival (cf. Study No. 18). Yet the words are applied to Christ! Moreover, the statement commences with the emphatic expression 'I am' (cf. Study No. 54), which comes ultimately from Exod. 3.14.

The further assertion that He is 'the living one' reminds us that God is so often described as 'the living God' in the Old Testament (e.g. Josh. 3.10; Psa. 42.2; 84.2). It was because He is the incarnation of the living God that Christ could not be held by death but triumphed gloriously over it.

A thought : I may never see such a vision on earth but I may use John's record of it to expand my view of Him.

90 : The Glory of God the Creator

Revelation 4

Samuel Chadwick, a great Principal of Cliff College, had a series of Bible passages which he used at particular times in his own private devotions. Every Sunday he read Rev. **4** and **5**. Why did he do this? Surely it was because praise is the highest activity of the redeemed man or woman, and we gain here some insight into the praise of heaven to stimulate our praise on earth. Indeed as the vision of these two chapters unfolds we become aware that we are not simply hearing heaven's praises but those of the whole creation. As you seek to imagine the scene do not let your mind be content with a cramped picture but let it be vast, as vast as the very universe itself!

Chapter **4** could well have come out of the pages of the Old Testament. Verses 1–6a remind us of passages like Exod. **19** and Ezek. **1**. We cannot enter into a discussion of all the detail but if the twenty-four elders are (as many think) representative of the people of God in the Old Testament and the New, then we have one item here which takes us beyond the Old Testament perspective. The four living creatures seem to partake of characteristics of the beings described in Ezek. **1** and **10**, and Isa. **6**. Like the seraphim of Isa. **6** they utter a threefold ascription of holiness to God (see Study No. 41). They are often regarded as symbolizing the subjection of all nature to God. The two groups join together in harmony and the elders extol God as the great Creator of all. It is there that all our thought about God begins. Our attention should be drawn away from everything else and we should worship the one true and living God. This was the message of the Old Testament.

> 'All things praise Thee, Lord most high; heaven and
>   earth and sea and sky.
> All were for Thy glory made, that Thy greatness,
>   thus displayed,
> Should all worship bring to Thee; all things praise
>   Thee : Lord, may we.'
>
> (George William Conder)

91 : The Glory of God the Redeemer

Revelation 5

The vision of ch. 4 is continued here. The scroll of human
destiny appears in the hand of God, and One only is worthy
to open it. John is being instructed by one of the elders who
calls on him to look at the Lion of Judah (5, cf. Gen. 49.9;
Isa. 11.1, 10). He has conquered all the enemies declared in
the book of destiny to be under judgement, and so His work
has prepared for their judgement.

But when John looks, instead of a Lion, he sees a Lamb
(6). He has apparently not seen Him earlier in the vision.
'None but an inspired composer of heavenly visions would
ever have thought of it. When earth-bound men want symbols
of power they conjure up mighty beasts and birds of prey. . . .
It is only the Kingdom of Heaven that would dare to use as
its symbol of might, not the Lion for which John was looking, but the helpless Lamb, and, at that, a slain Lamb'
(J. P. Love). Although the Lamb is a slain, sacrificial Lamb,
yet it is standing, and so is risen and exalted. It has 'seven
horns', suggestive of perfect power, which God alone possesses, and so He rightly takes His place in the midst of the
throne (7.17). It also has 'seven eyes, which are the seven
spirits of God sent out into all the earth', and so we are
made aware of the fact that through the perfect Divine Spirit
He can be, not only in the presence of God, but everywhere
also with His people.

Now the praise begins again, but this time it has a new
note; the praise of the Lamb is joined with the praise of
God (13). This is doubly significant in a book where angels,
as creatures, refuse worship (22.8 f.). Praise is offered for His
glorious redemption.

The doctrine of the Trinity is no piece of speculative
theology far removed from the real concerns of the spiritual
life, but represents the only faithful understanding of the
biblical facts. The Triune God should be, not only the high
Subject of the believer's thought, but the One before whom
he lies prostrate in adoration and in whose service he finds
the reason for his creation and redemption.

'From all that dwell below the skies let the Creator's praise arise: Hallelujah!

Let the Redeemer's name be sung through every land, by every tongue: Hallelujah!'

(*Isaac Watts*)

Questions and themes for study and discussion on Studies 84–91

1. Study the language of fullness as applied to God in the Ephesian letter (1.23; 3.19; 4.13; 5.18).

2. Trace the use of the term 'Saviour' elsewhere in the Pastoral Epistles.

3. Study the doctrine of the Holy Spirit in the remainder of the letter to the Hebrews.

4. Consider the devotional implications of 1 Pet. 1.1–12.

5. Does the use of a doxology to Christ imply anything about the nature of His Person (Rev. 1.5 f.)?

6. In a good reference Bible, study the Old Testament background to Rev. 1 in more detail and ponder its doctrinal significance.

7. Calvin's 'Institutes of the Christian Religion' deals with the knowledge of God the Creator before going on to the knowledge of God the Redeemer. Why is this necessary?

8. How has my worship of God been enriched by the knowledge that I may come to the Father through the Son and in the Spirit?